WILLIAM WORDSWORTH

WORDSWORTH

Poetry & Prose

With Essays by

COLERIDGE   HAZLITT

DE QUINCEY

With an Introduction by

DAVID NICHOL SMITH

and Notes

OXFORD

AT THE CLARENDON PRESS

THE frontispiece, a reproduction of a portrait painted at Nether Stowey in 1798 by W. Shuter, is taken by permission from the photogravure published by Messrs. William George's Sons of Bristol.

The notes are by A. M. D. Hughes and the Editor.

FIRST PUBLISHED 1921
REPRINTED 1923, 1924, 1928, 1933, 1937
1942, 1948 (TWICE), 1952, 1956, 1960
1968, 1969

PRINTED IN GREAT BRITAIN
AT THE UNIVERSITY PRESS, OXFORD
BY VIVIAN RIDLER
PRINTER TO THE UNIVERSITY

CONTENTS

iv CONTENTS

loss of
m

INTRODUCTION

WORDSWORTH'S early poems were a challenge to the critics. He professed to publish some of them as an experiment ; he did not conceal that he hoped to lead poetry into new paths, or back into old paths. ' They who have been accustomed to the gaudiness and inane phraseology of many modern writers,' he said in his preface to *Lyrical Ballads*, ' if they persist in reading this book to its conclusion, will, no doubt, frequently have to struggle with feelings of strangeness and awkwardness ; they will look round for poetry, and will be induced to inquire by what species of courtesy these attempts can be permitted to assume that title.' He was prepared for opposition, but it was stronger and more persistent than he had hoped. Many poets have had to win their way through cold neglect to the full recognition of their powers. But Wordsworth was never neglected ; each new volume of his poems was the occasion of merriment or amazement. All the while, in the remoteness of his Cumbrian home, unaffected by what the reviewers might say of him in London or Edinburgh, and assured of the truth of what he said and how he said it, Wordsworth held to his even course. He was at his greatest as a poet between the publication of *Lyrical Ballads* in 1798 and the publication of *The Excursion* in 1814. During the remaining thirty-six years of his life he wrote much, but only occasionally did he recapture the life and the vision of his great creative period. The tide of critical opinion turned strongly in his favour just as this period was passing. ' Every great and original writer, in proportion as he is great or original,' he had said, ' must create the taste by which he is to be relished ; he must teach the art by which he is to be seen.' He succeeded in creating the taste, and the honours which were due to him for what he had done in his youth were fully paid in his old age.

He had never lacked readers who welcomed the novel and unique quality of his work, as he expected, with more than common pleasure. But the best pieces of deliberate criticism, at once the most appreciative and judicial, date from the time when his fame was established. Of the pieces which he himself might have read, three stand out prominently from the rest—the twenty-second chapter of Coleridge's *Biographia Literaria* (1817), an essay by Hazlitt in his *Spirit of the Age or Contemporary Portraits* (1823), and a magazine article by De Quincey (1845). They were written from different points of view, and with different purposes, but together they represent contemporary opinion at its best, and they exhibit the difficulties, as well as the satisfaction, which readers at all times have found in Wordsworth's poetry.

Coleridge and Wordsworth had both owed much to each other. Their friendship in 1797 and 1798, when they lived near the Quantock hills in Somerset, Coleridge at Nether Stowey and Wordsworth about three miles distant at Alfoxden, is one of the great friendships in English literature. It immediately bore fruit in their *Lyrical Ballads*. Both had written much already and were feeling their way to their poetic methods when their active intercourse gave them the confidence that comes from appreciation and encouragement. Wordsworth's definite adoption of what may be called his poetic creed belongs to these years. Different as they were in temperament and intellectual gifts, each had met in the other the man who could lead him to the fullest and most individual expression of his thought. Coleridge's admiration was unbounded. ' Wordsworth ', he said, ' is a very great man, the only man to whom at all

times and in all modes of excellence I feel myself inferior.'
If Wordsworth did not speak of Coleridge with the same
continuous enthusiasm, it was only because he was naturally
more reticent, and less easily moved ; but on more than
one occasion he described Coleridge as ' the only *wonderful*
man that I ever knew ', and in his old age, when Coleridge
was dead, he recalled

> The rapt One, of the godlike forehead,
> The heaven-eyed creature,

in a passage that glows with the recollection of the years
they had spent together. Almost from the first they found
that their methods were too divergent to allow them to
collaborate on the same poem. They produced their
Lyrical Ballads under the stimulus of their close companion-
ship, but their poems were in their characteristic styles ;
the first was *The Ancient Mariner* and the last *Tintern
Abbey*.

When about twenty years later Coleridge wrote his *Biographia Literaria* he had to speak of the man who had meant
more to him than any one else while he was writing his own
greatest poetry ; and as in the interval they had come to mean
very much less to each other, for they had long assimilated
all that the other could give, the balance of his judgement
was not disturbed by the old enthusiasm. Coleridge was at
this time leading his erratic, brilliant, disappointing life in
London. He had abandoned poetry for philosophy ; he
lectured on poetry, he wrote for the periodicals, he talked.
He was now able to take an outside view of Wordsworth's
poetry, and to speak of it without prejudice. From the
beginning he had felt that its greatness was injured by
clearly marked types of faults. These he now stated to the
public, judicially and for the most part incontrovertibly.
But he also held, and with reason, that no one understood
Wordsworth better than he did, and he showed, as judicially
and incontrovertibly, on what this greatness rested. ' In

imaginative power, he stands nearest of all modern writers to Shakespeare and Milton, and yet in a kind perfectly unborrowed and his own : ' this was his deliberate and his final opinion. The whole passage—a complete chapter of the *Biographia Literaria*—is an excursion into a kind of criticism that Coleridge did not usually practise. His subtle mind never showed to better advantage than when he discussed theoretical questions, as in the earlier chapter on Wordsworth's views on the language of poetry ; and his imaginative sympathy makes him one of the great masters of exposition and interpretation, as in some of his lectures on Shakespeare. In his estimate of Wordsworth he proceeds on the method of separating the defects and excellences, classifying them, and balancing them. It is a kind of criticism that in all but the most skilful hands is liable to be so formal as to become soulless. In Coleridge's, nothing could be soulless. Whatever method he had adopted he must have spoken of Wordsworth's poetry with privileged knowledge of its purpose, and with real understanding of its spirit.

Hazlitt's criticism of Wordsworth is of another kind. His essay is, in the main, a portrait or character study— one of a series on twenty-four of the more notable men of his time, all chosen as representing in their different ways ' the spirit of the age '. He had first met Wordsworth in the spring of 1798 when he was the guest of Coleridge at Nether Stowey, and they had spent some days together a few years later when Wordsworth was settled at Grasmere. Thereafter they appear to have met only once. Hazlitt never knew Wordsworth intimately, but he had been able to form a clear idea of his person and character, and he had always been interested in his poetry since the day when he heard Coleridge read some of the *Lyrical Ballads* from the manuscript before they were sent to the printer. He was a man of many interests. His taste in literature was formed mainly on the study of the greater English and French writers of the seventeenth and eighteenth centuries. He had trained as a painter and was not unsuccessful in portraiture, he had written on philosophy and politics, he had been a parliamentary reporter and theatrical critic, he had done much work of one kind or another for the booksellers before he definitely adopted the profession of critic and essayist. He was more a man of the world than either Wordsworth or Coleridge, and he viewed the literary ferment of his day without any prepossessions. Of much of the work of his contemporaries he was severely critical. ' I am nothing if not critical,' he said of himself, quoting Iago. He spoke his mind with perfect frankness ; he could not write without being frank. If he allowed full play to his enthusiasms, and they were many, when he spoke of earlier writers, he was incapable of idealizing any living man. ' I always believe you when you praise, not always when you condemn ' is a comment which he passed on himself in an imaginary dialogue. He paints his contemporaries as he sees them, and makes their faults and their foibles an important part of the picture. So he tells us that Wordsworth ' has some difficulty to contend with the hebetude of his intellect ' ; that his mind is ' obtuse except as it is the organ and the receptacle of accumulated feelings'; that he is a supreme egotist; that his high and severe standard of poetry ' admits of nothing below, scarcely of anything above himself '; that ' to one class of readers he appears sublime, to another (and we fear the largest) ridiculous '. Such statements as these are necessary to Hazlitt's method in portraiture. He takes account of everything that the scope of a brief essay will allow ; there is nothing that he would conceal. And for this reason those readers who are not Wordsworth's ' determined partisans ', who find things in his poetry that jar on their taste, who cannot harmonize their minds to his, who look for another

kind of pleasure than he can give, are likely to find more
satisfaction in Hazlitt than in any other of Wordsworth's
great critics. But finding so much with which they agree,
they may be induced to consider if they cannot agree with
it all. And if there is any one passage in Hazlitt's essay
which may be selected as representative of it all, it is this :
' He has described all these objects in a way and with an
intensity of feeling that no one else had done before him,
and has given a new view or aspect of nature. He is in this
sense the most original poet now living, and the one whose
writings could the least be spared, for they have no substitute elsewhere.'

In contrast to Coleridge and Hazlitt, De Quincey did
' intellectual homage '. In his first year as an undergraduate at Oxford he had ventured to address to Wordsworth a letter of fervent admiration, and a few years later
he had made his home at Grasmere in the hope of enjoying
Wordsworth's society. He has himself described how he
did not enjoy it as much as he expected ; he found the poet
incapable of forming any strong attachment outside his
family circle, and unwilling to allow his mind to feed on
anything but what it provided for itself. But the sense of
discipleship was never wholly lost, and the influence which
it had once exerted was never concealed. In the last of
several essays devoted wholly or in part to Wordsworth,
De Quincey explained his debt to Wordsworth's poetry.
He treated it as a great body of literature to be studied for
its own sake, without relation to the life of its author or
the age when it was written. He had already written so
much about Wordsworth the man that in this essay he at
last attempted to forget the man and to see only the poetry.
It is an exercise—he says it was his first—in impersonal
criticism. ' Wordsworth ' is to all intents only a name for
a remarkable collection of poems with common characteris-
tics, all written from the same standpoint and enforcing

the same lesson. The permanent value of these poems as a whole is given by De Quincey in a sentence. They have 'brought many a truth into life both for the eye and for the understanding, which previously had slumbered indistinctly for all men'. It is much the same idea that Pope had expressed in his *Essay on Criticism* when he spoke of

Something whose truth convinc'd at sight we find,
That gives us back the image of our mind.

The idea is as old as Horace. De Quincey gives it in his own exuberant richly coloured style, and illustrates it from Wordsworth's poetry. It is the final test of great poetry. The author whose fame will endure is 'not he that perplexes men by truths drawn from fountains of absolute novelty—truths as yet unsunned, and from that cause obscure ; but he that awakens into illuminated consciousness ancient lineaments of truth long slumbering in the mind'. He has seen and felt what other men may see and feel, but he has seen it more clearly or felt it more keenly ; he has found a deeper meaning in it, or realized it in new aspects ; and he enriches our experience by putting us into fuller possession of the wealth amid which we move, but is wealth only in so far as our minds are able to receive it. Judged by this test, Wordsworth seemed to De Quincey to be the most original poet of his day. In meditative poetry he was without a rival since Shakespeare.

When De Quincey said that Wordsworth's poetry is distinguished by the extent of its 'sympathy with what is *really* permanent in human feelings' he did little more than put in his own words what the poet himself had said again and again.

My theme
No other than the very heart of man,

he says in *The Prelude.* In *Michael* he tells how he was led on to think

On man, the heart of man, and human life.

The motive of *The Old Cumberland Beggar* is that

> We have all of us one human heart.

Wordsworth is concerned above all with the essential qualities or what he calls ' the primary laws ' of our nature, and these he maintained could be best studied in the ordinary circumstances of commonplace life. He saw

> little worthy or sublime
> In what the Historian's pen so much delights
> To blazon.

The simpler and more natural workings of the heart may be obscured in great political crises or in events and careers that dazzle the imagination. He distrusts whatever dazzles ; he distrusts whatever is abnormal. The stories which he tells are of the simplest, a mere setting for his meditations on some aspect of ordinary human nature. Nothing that he has written is more full of incident or more rapid in movement than his *Song at the Feast of Brougham Castle*, but the purpose of the whole poem lies in its quiet ending. He said in his *Hart-leap Well* that

> The moving accident is not my trade ;
> To freeze the blood I have no ready arts.

He has also repeatedly said, and notably in *The Prelude*, where he found his trade. He found it in

> the vulgar forms of present things,
> The actual world of our familiar days.

There is no more striking passage on the subjects he chooses for his poetry than three short stanzas in the prologue to his *Peter Bell*. They are an echo of the disagreement which caused him to part company with Coleridge in the composition of *The Ancient Mariner*. How is the poet to deal with the marvellous ? Is he to assume its existence and then to relate it to actual life ? Is he to begin with incidents and agents that are supernatural, but to treat them as if they were real, and so to make his poem a symbol or reflection of the reality ? Or is he to begin with the matter of everyday experience, and to see in it what the eye usually fails to see amid the busy cares of life, to rise from the firm basis of simple fact to what is beyond and above it ? There was only one way for Wordsworth.

> Long have I loved what I behold,
> The night that calms, the day that cheers ;
> The common growth of mother-earth
> Suffices me—her tears, her mirth,
> Her humblest mirth and tears.
>
> The dragon's wing, the magic ring,
> I shall not covet for my dower,
> If I along that lowly way
> With sympathetic heart may stray,
> And with a soul of power.
>
> These given, what more need I desire
> To stir, to soothe, or elevate ?
> What nobler prospects than the mind
> May in life's daily prospect find,
> May find or there create ?

Wordsworth had never any wish to escape from the commonplaces of life. He accepted them all, and viewed them with a calmness and a courage that could never be shaken.

There was nothing too humble for Wordsworth ; he only required that it should be familiar. But the subjects that he nominally chooses may not be the real subjects of his poems. The titles afford as a rule little clue to what the poems contain. Wordsworth does not value anything for itself so much as for what it can tell us of ourselves. There was no need for him to search for material outside the beaten track when everywhere around him things were ' for ever speaking ' and he had only to listen. He can find ' a tale in every thing ', and he shows his readers how they too may find it in what they pass by as worthless or insignificant in the hurry of their daily pursuits. He has

> among least things
> An under-sense of greatest ; sees the parts
> As parts, but with a feeling of the whole.

His poem called *The Small Celandine* is a poem on the human lot.

> Thanks to the human heart by which we live,
> Thanks to its tenderness, its joys, and fears,
> To me the meanest flower that blows can give
> Thoughts that do often lie too deep for tears.

Wordsworth could not be expected to take any interest in plot for its own sake. More than this, he took little interest in the study of character as it is generally understood—in the traits which distinguish one man from another. He finds his theme in the qualities that are common to all men. The persons of his stories are a leech-gatherer, a schoolmaster, an old shepherd and his son, or an aged beggar. It does not matter what names he gives them. They have no habits of mind that are necessarily connected with their occupations ; they are not drawn as clearly marked types ; much less are they individuals. They are simply men, old or young, or women, or children, as nature makes them, and as little affected as may be by the conventions of society.

He tried to abandon, as far as he could, the conventions of the language of poetry, using instead ' a selection of the language really spoken by men '. Here, too, he sought the essential and the permanent as much as in the matter of the poems. Unfortunately, in his preface to *Lyrical Ballads*, he approached the difficult question of poetic diction too much in the manner of a challenge, and without fully considering all that was involved. Coleridge, who was a greater adept in theoretical discussion, had no difficulty in showing the weak points in the argument ; and unfriendly critics have not failed to take their opportunity. But the diction of Wordsworth's poetry would have raised no questions if he had not himself directed attention to it. He could not keep in every poem to the maxims which he stated somewhat unwarily in this early preface ; no poet can always use the language of ordinary speech. He meant to plead for simplicity, and in the ardour of his attack on ' gaudiness and inane phraseology ' he had allowed his plea, sound in itself and not untimely, to develop into a provocative manifesto. What has never to be forgotten is that the plea was only a consequence, and a necessary consequence, of the guiding principle of his poetry, and that in some of his greatest passages he does use the language really spoken by men.

He said of his poems that ' the feeling therein developed gives importance to the action and situation, and not the action and situation to the feeling '. He is not a narrative poet, as the title is commonly understood ; and he has little capacity or liking for the dramatic, though in his youth he wrote a tragedy. The simple facts of life become the subject of his poetry only as they appeal to his heart, and he views them at rest, or moving in their slow and ordered course. He described poetry as taking its origin in ' emotion recollected in tranquillity '. This may not be true of all poetry, but it is true of his own. He was

> not used to make
> A present joy the matter of a song.

He rather writes of his memories. The voice of the cuckoo awakens recollections of his schoolboy days, and he listens till he can ' beget that golden time again '. A host of daffodils seen one bright April morning dancing in the

wind by the margin of a lake are a recurring embodiment
of the spirit of joy each time they

> flash upon that inward eye
> Which is the bliss of solitude.

His memories are memories of feeling, to be indulged and
examined in long periods of rapt meditative calm. He tells
us in *The Waggoner* how they sometimes came unbidden
and demanded to be put on record.

> Nor is it I who play the part,
> But a shy spirit in my heart,
> That comes and goes—will sometimes leap
> From hiding-places ten years deep ;
> Or haunts me with familiar face,
> Returning, like a ghost unlaid,
> Until the debt I owe be paid.

There were times when, ' in a wise passiveness,' he found
he could learn more through the feelings than ' all the
sages ' could teach him ; the ordinary intellectual pursuits
that require ' years of toiling reason ' seemed to him to
shut off one of the great sources of our knowledge. It
would be difficult to find a poet who has told us more about
the conditions of the composition of his poetry than Wordsworth has, and there can be no better statement of his
method and aim than a series of quotations from his own
writings. They would be chosen mainly from his early
poems—from the poems that were written when he had
found his strength and had just shaped his creed ; and
they would be found to supplement each other so as to form
a compact body of doctrine. Every loyal interpretation of
his poetry as a whole must be based on them, and Wordsworth demands loyalty.

All that was vital in his knowledge had been revealed
through the feelings. He did not indulge

> sensations sweet,
> Felt in the blood, and felt along the heart,

for their own sake, but as a means to an end ; they provided
the conditions in which knowledge would come. Only
as the Imagination was then brought into play could he
' see into the life of things '. Imagination, as Wordsworth
understood it, is the power that leads us to the truth. It is
at once vision and reconstruction. It brings the mind into
unison with the object of contemplation, disengages the
forces or principles that govern it, and interprets it in the
light of these. On the other hand he thought of Fancy as
dealing superficially with the outward forms or manifestations of things and depending on the rapidity and profusion
with which she scatters her thoughts and images. ' Fancy ',
he says, ' is given to quicken and to beguile the temporal
part of our nature, Imagination to incite and to support the
eternal.' They could not be rigidly separated, for each at
times would call the other to its aid. But the distinction
was clear enough for Wordsworth to adopt it in the arrangement of his first collected edition, where there is a group of
' Poems of the Fancy ' and another of ' Poems of the
Imagination '. In the former he placed such poems as
To the Daisy and *The Green Linnet* ; in the latter, *To the
Cuckoo, Nutting,* ' I wandered lonely as a cloud,' *Resolution
and Independence,* and *Tintern Abbey.*

Nature was to Wordsworth a living soul that reveals
herself alike in the movements of the stars, the yearnings
of the heart, the sleep of a great city, or the decay of
a flower.

> To every Form of being is assigned
> An *active* Principle : howe'er removed
> From sense and observation, it subsists
> In all things, in all natures ; in the stars
> Of azure heaven, the unenduring clouds,
> In flower and tree, in every pebbly stone
> That paves the brooks, the stationary rocks,
> The moving waters, and the invisible air.

> Whate'er exists hath properties that spread
> Beyond itself, communicating good,
> A simple blessing, or with evil mixed ;
> Spirit that knows no insulated spot,
> No chasm, no solitude ; from link to link
> It circulates, the Soul of all the worlds.
>
> *The Excursion IX.*

His poetry makes no division between man and the world in which he lives. He thinks of all created things, human or inanimate, as parts of one great whole, filling their appointed place, moving in their established order. He is our greatest nature poet because he is the poet of more than external nature ; he is, in a higher degree, the poet of man. No other poet is more consistently original and faithful in his pictures of what the eye can see, more luminous in his interpretation of it. But he could never dissociate it from the human heart.

One purpose runs throughout all his poems. He never stated it more simply than in a casual sentence in a letter which he wrote when his long career was drawing to its close. ' What I should myself most value in my attempts ' he there defined as being ' the spirituality with which I have endeavoured to invest the material universe, and the moral relations under which I have wished to exhibit its most ordinary appearances '.

WORDSWORTH'S LIFE

1770. William Wordsworth born at Cockermouth, Cumberland, April 7.

1778–87. At Hawkshead Grammar School. His mother dies, 1778; his father, 1783.

1787–91. At St. John's College, Cambridge.

1790. First visit to France: walking tour of fourteen weeks in France and Switzerland.

1791–2. Second visit to France: Paris (November), Orleans, Blois, Paris (October).

1793. *An Evening Walk* and *Descriptive Sketches* published. Walking tour by Salisbury, Stonehenge, Bristol, and Tintern Abbey to Wales.

1795. Settles with his sister Dorothy at Racedown, Dorset. Meets Coleridge.

1797. Visits Coleridge at Nether Stowey, Somerset; leaves Racedown and settles at Alfoxden, near Nether Stowey.

1798. *Lyrical Ballads* (September). Visit to Germany (September 1798–April 1799).

1799. Settles at Dove Cottage, Townend, Grasmere (his home till 1808).

1802. Visit to Calais (August). Marries Mary Hutchinson at Brompton, near Scarborough, October 4.

1803. First tour in Scotland. Meets Walter Scott.

1805. His sailor brother John drowned at sea.

1806. Lives at Coleorton, Leicestershire, from October 1806 to the summer of 1807.

1807. *Poems in Two Volumes.*

1808. Moves from Dove Cottage to Allan Bank, Grasmere (his home till 1811).

1809. *The Convention of Cintra* (see note, p. 212).

1811. Moves from Allan Bank to the Rectory, Grasmere (his home till 1813).

1812. Death of two of his children.

1813. Settles at Rydal Mount, his home for the rest of his life. Appointed Stamp-Distributor for Westmoreland.

1814. Second tour in Scotland. *The Excursion.*

1815. *Poems*, two vols. (first collected edition). *The White Doe of Rylstone* (begun 1807).

1816. *A Letter to a Friend of Robert Burns. Thanksgiving Ode.*

1818. *Two Addresses to the Freeholders of Westmoreland.*

1819. *Peter Bell* (written 1798). *The Waggoner* (written 1805).

1820. *The River Duddon, a Series of Sonnets. Miscellaneous Poems,* four vols. (second collected edition, revised). *The Excursion* (second edition, revised). Fifth visit to the Continent: Switzerland, the Italian Lakes, Paris (July–November).

1822. *Memorials of a Tour on the Continent, 1820. Ecclesiastical Sketches* (called *Sonnets* in 1837).

1823. Sixth visit to the Continent : tour in the Netherlands.

1827. *Poetical Works*, five vols. (third collected edition, revised).

1828. Seventh visit to the Continent : tour up the Rhine.

1829. Tour in Ireland.

1830. Rides from Lancaster to Cambridge, 'a solitary equestrian'.

1831. Third tour in Scotland : visits Scott at Abbotsford (see note, p. 207).

1832. *Poetical Works*, four vols. (fourth collected edition, revised).

1835. *Yarrow Revisited, and other Poems. A Guide through the District of the Lakes in the North of England* (see note, p. 212).

1836–7. *Poetical Works*, six vols. (fifth collected edition, revised).

1838. *The Sonnets of William Wordsworth, collected in one volume.*

1841. Revisits Alfoxden and Tintern.

1842. *Poems, chiefly of Early and Late Years* (called ' Volume VII '). Resigns post of Stamp-Distributor for Westmoreland; receives a pension of £300 from the Civil List.

1843. Appointed Poet Laureate in succession to Southey. Dictates notes on his poems to Miss Fenwick.

1844. *Kendal and Windermere Railway : Two Letters reprinted from the Morning Post.*

1845. *Poems*, one vol. (sixth collected edition, revised).

1847. *Ode, performed in the Senate-House, Cambridge.*

1849–50. *Poetical Works*, six vols, giving his final revision of the text.

1850. Dies at Rydal Mount (April 23). *The Prelude* (begun 1799, completed 1805, revised 1839, published posthumously).

From COLERIDGE'S

BIOGRAPHIA LITERARIA

I CANNOT here enter into a detailed examination of Mr. Wordsworth's works ; but I will attempt to give the main results of my own judgement, after an acquaintance of many years, and repeated perusals. And though to appreciate the defects of a great mind it is necessary to understand previously its characteristic excellences, yet I have already expressed myself with sufficient fulness, to preclude most of the ill effects that might arise from my pursuing a contrary arrangement. I will therefore commence with what I deem the prominent *defects* of his poems hitherto pub- 10 lished.

The first *characteristic, though only occasional* defect, which I appear to myself to find in these poems is the INCONSTANCY of the *style*. Under this name I refer to the sudden and unprepared transitions from lines or sentences of peculiar felicity (at all events striking and original) to a style, not only unimpassioned but undistinguished. He sinks too often and too abruptly to that style which I should place in the second division of language, dividing it into the three species ; *first*, that which is peculiar to poetry ; *second*, 20 that which is only proper in prose ; and *third*, the neutral or common to both. There have been works, such as Cowley's Essay on Cromwell, in which prose and verse are intermixed (not as in the Consolation of Boetius, or the Argenis of Barclay, by the insertion of poems supposed to have been spoken or composed on occasions previously related in prose, but) the poet passing from one to the other, as the nature of the thoughts or his own feelings dictated. Yet

this mode of composition does not satisfy a cultivated taste.
There is something unpleasant in the being thus obliged to
alternate states of feeling so dissimilar, and this too in a
species of writing, the pleasure from which is in part derived
from the preparation and previous expectation of the reader.
A portion of that awkwardness is felt which hangs upon the
introduction of songs in our modern comic operas ; and to
prevent which the judicious Metastasio (as to whose exquisite *taste* there can be no hesitation, whatever doubts may
10 be entertained as to his *poetic genius*) uniformly placed the
ARIA at the end of the scene, at the same time that he almost
always raises and impassions the style of the recitative
immediately preceding. Even in real life, the difference is
great and evident between words used as the *arbitrary marks*
of thought, our smooth market-coin of intercourse, with the
image and superscription worn out by currency ; and those
which convey pictures either borrowed from *one* outward
object to enliven and particularize some *other* ; or used
allegorically to body forth the inward state of the person
20 speaking ; or such as are at least the exponents of his peculiar turn and unusual extent of faculty. So much so indeed,
that in the social circles of private life we often find a striking
use of the latter put a stop to the general flow of conversation, and by the excitement arising from concentered attention produce a sort of damp and interruption for some
minutes after. But in the perusal of works of literary *art*,
we *prepare* ourselves for such language ; and the business
of the writer, like that of a painter whose subject requires
unusual splendour and prominence, is so to raise the lower
30 and neutral tints, that what in a different style would be
the *commanding* colours, are here used as the means of that
gentle *degradation* requisite in order to produce the effect
of a *whole*. Where this is not achieved in a poem, the
metre merely reminds the reader of his claims in order to
disappoint them ; and where this defect occurs frequently,

his feelings are alternately startled by anticlimax and hyper-climax.

[Instances of 'this *disharmony* of style' are here given from *The Blind Highland Boy*, *The Emigrant Mother*, and *To a Skylark* (1805) ; and finally from *Resolution and Independence*.]

> Close by a pond, upon the further side,
> He stood alone ; a minute's space, I guess,
> I watch'd him, he continuing motionless :
> To the pool's further margin then I drew,
> He being all the while before me full in view.

Compare this with the repetition of the same image, in the next stanza but two.

> And, still as I drew near with gentle pace,   10
> Beside the little pond or moorish flood
> Motionless as a cloud the old man stood,
> That heareth not the loud winds as they call,
> And moveth altogether, if it move at all.

Or lastly, the second of the three following stanzas, compared both with the first and the third.

> My former thoughts returned ; the fear that kills ;
> And hope that is unwilling to be fed ;
> Cold, pain, and labour, and all fleshly ills ;
> And mighty poets in their misery dead.
> But now, perplex'd by what the old man had said,   20
> My question eagerly did I renew,
> ' How is it that you live, and what is it you do ? '
> He with a smile did then his words repeat ;
> And said, that gathering leeches far and wide
> He travell'd ; stirring thus about his feet
> The waters of the ponds where they abide.
> ' Once I could meet with them on every side,
> ' But they have dwindled long by slow decay ;
> ' Yet still I persevere, and find them where I may.'   30
> While he was talking thus, the lonely place,
> The old man's shape, and speech, all troubled me :
> In my mind's eye I seemed to see him pace
> About the weary moors continually,
> Wandering about alone and silently.

Indeed this fine poem is *especially* characteristic of the author. There is scarce a defect or excellence in his writings of which it would not present a specimen. But it would be unjust not to repeat that this defect is only occasional. From a careful reperusal of the two volumes of poems, I doubt whether the objectionable passages would amount in the whole to one hundred lines ; not the eighth part of the number of pages. In the EXCURSION the feeling of incongruity is seldom excited by the diction of any passage considered
10 in itself, but by the sudden superiority of some other passage forming the context.

The second defect I can generalize with tolerable accuracy, if the reader will pardon an uncouth and new-coined word. There is, I should say, not seldom a *matter-of-factness* in certain poems. This may be divided into, *first*, a laborious minuteness and fidelity in the representation of objects, and their positions, as they appeared to the poet himself ; *secondly*, the insertion of accidental circumstances, in order to the full explanation of his living characters, their disposi-
20 tions and actions ; which circumstances might be necessary to establish the probability of a statement in real life, where nothing is taken for granted by the hearer, but appear superfluous in poetry, where the reader is willing to believe for his own sake. To this *accidentality* I object, as contravening the essence of poetry, which Aristotle pronounces to be σπουδαιότατον καὶ φιλοσοφώτατον γένος, the most intense, weighty, and philosophical product of human art ; adding, as the *reason*, that it is the most catholic and abstract. The following passage from Davenant's prefatory letter to Hobbs
30 well expresses this truth. ' When I considered the actions which I meant to describe, (those inferring the persons), I was again persuaded rather to choose those of a former age, than the present ; and in a century so far removed, as might preserve me from their improper examinations, who know not the requisites of a poem, nor how much pleasure

they lose, (and even the pleasures of heroic poesy are not unprofitable), who take away the liberty of a poet, and fetter his feet in the shackles of an historian. For why should a poet doubt in story to mend the intrigues of fortune by more delightful conveyances of probable fictions, because austere historians have entered into bond to truth ?—an obligation which were in poets as foolish and unnecessary, as is the bondage of false martyrs, who lie in chains for a mistaken opinion. *But by this I would imply, that truth narrative and past is the idol of historians (who worship a dead* 10 *thing), and truth operative, and by effects continually alive, is the mistress of poets, who hath not her existence in matter, but in reason.'*

It must be some strong motive (as, for instance, that the description was necessary to the intelligibility of the tale) which could induce me to describe in a number of verses what a draughtsman could present to the eye with incomparably greater satisfaction by half a dozen strokes of his pencil, or the painter with as many touches of his brush. Such descriptions too often occasion in the mind 20 of a reader, who is determined to understand his author, a feeling of labour, not very dissimilar to that with which he would construct a diagram, line by line, for a long geometrical proposition. It seems to be like taking the pieces of a dissected map out of its box. We first look at one part, and then at another, then join and dove-tail them ; and when the successive acts of attention have been completed, there is a retrogressive effort of mind to behold it as a whole. The poet should paint to the imagination, not to the fancy ; and I know no happier case to exemplify the distinction 30 between these two faculties. Master-pieces of the former mode of poetic painting abound in the writings of Milton, ex. gr.

The fig-tree ; not that kind for fruit renown'd,
But such as at this day, to Indians known,

In Malabar or Decan spreads her arms
Branching so broad and long, that in the ground
The bended twigs take root, *and daughters grow*
About the mother tree, a pillar'd shade
High over-arch'd, and ECHOING WALKS BETWEEN :
There oft the Indian Herdsman, shunning heat,
Shelters in cool, and tends his pasturing herds
At loop holes cut through thickest shade.

MILTON *P. L.* ix. 1001.

This is *creation* rather than *painting*, or if painting, yet
10 such, and with such co-presence of the whole picture flash'd
at once upon the eye, as the sun paints in a camera obscura.
But the poet must likewise understand and command what
Bacon calls the *vestigia communia* of the senses, the latency
of all in each, and more especially as by a magical *penna
duplex*, the excitement of vision by sound and the exponents of sound.   Thus ' THE ECHOING WALKS BETWEEN '
may be almost said to reverse the fable in tradition of
the head of Memnon, in the Egyptian statue.   Such may
be deservedly entitled the *creative words* in the world of
20 imagination.

The second division respects an apparent minute adhe-
rence to *matter-of-fact* in characters and incidents ; *a bio-
graphical* attention to probability, and an *anxiety* of explanation and retrospect.   Under this head I shall deliver, with
no feigned diffidence, the results of my best reflection on the
great point of controversy between Mr. Wordsworth and
his objectors ; namely, on THE CHOICE OF HIS CHARACTERS.
I have already declared and, I trust, justified, my utter
dissent from the mode of argument which his critics have
30 hitherto employed.   To *their* question, Why did you choose
such a character, or a character from such a rank of life ?
the poet might in my opinion fairly retort : why with the
conception of my character did you make wilful choice of
mean or ludicrous associations not furnished by me, but
supplied from your own sickly and fastidious feelings ? How

was it, indeed, probable, that such arguments could have any weight with an author, whose plan, whose guiding principle, and main object it was to attack and subdue that state of association, which leads us to place the chief value on those things in which man DIFFERS from man, and to forget or disregard the high dignities which belong to HUMAN NATURE, the sense and the feeling which *may* be, and *ought* to be, found in *all* ranks ?   The feelings with which, as Christians, we contemplate a mixed congregation rising or kneeling before their common Maker, Mr. Words- worth would have us entertain at *all* times, as men, and as readers ; and by the excitement of this lofty yet prideless impartiality in *poetry*, he might hope to have encouraged its continuance in *real life*. The praise of good men be his ! In real life, and, I trust, even in my imagination, I honour a virtuous and wise man, without reference to the presence or absence of artificial advantages. Whether in the person of an armed baron, a laurel'd bard, &c., or of an old pedlar, or still older leech-gatherer, the same qualities of head and heart must claim the same reverence. And even in poetry I am not conscious that I have ever suffered my feelings to be disturbed or offended by any thoughts or images, which the poet himself has not presented.

But yet I object nevertheless and for the following reasons.   First, because the object in view, as an *immediate* object, belongs to the moral philosopher, and would be pursued, not only more appropriately, but in my opinion with far greater probability of success, in sermons or moral essays, than in an elevated poem. It seems, indeed, to destroy the main fundamental distinction, not only between a poem and prose, but even between philosophy and works of fiction, inasmuch as it proposes *truth* for its immediate object, instead of *pleasure*. Now till the blessed time shall come, when truth itself shall be pleasure, and both shall be so united as to be distinguishable in words only, not in feeling, it will remain the poet's office to proceed upon that state of association, which actually exists as *general* ; instead of attempting first to *make* it what it ought to be, and then to let the pleasure follow. But here is unfortunately a small *Hysteron-Proteron*. For the communication of pleasure is the introductory means by which alone the poet must expect to moralize his readers. Secondly : though I were to admit, for a moment, *this* argument to be groundless, yet how is the moral effect to be produced, by merely attaching the name of some low profession to powers which are *least* likely, and to qualities which are assuredly not *more* likely, to be found in it ? The poet, speaking in his own person, may at once delight and improve us by sentiments which teach us the independence of goodness, of wisdom, and even of genius, on the favours of fortune. And having made a due reverence before the throne of Antonine, he may bow with equal awe before Epictetus among his fellow-slaves—

> ——————————and rejoice
> In the plain presence of his dignity.

Who is not at once delighted and improved, when the POET Wordsworth himself exclaims,

> O many are the poets that are sown
> By Nature ; man endowed with highest gifts,
> The vision and the faculty divine,
> Yet wanting the accomplishment of verse,
> Nor having e'er, as life advanced, been led
> By circumstance to take unto the height
> The measure of themselves, these favour'd beings,
> All but a scatter'd few, live out their time
> Husbanding that which they possess within,
> And go to the grave unthought of. Strongest minds
> Are often those of whom the noisy world
> Hears least.
>
> EXCURSION, B. I.

To use a colloquial phrase, such sentiments, in such language, do one's heart good ; though I for my part, have not the fullest faith in the *truth* of the observation. On the contrary I believe the instances to be exceedingly rare ; and should feel almost as strong an objection to introduce such a character in a poetic fiction, as a pair of black swans on a lake in a fancy-landscape. When I think how many and how much better books than Homer, or even than Herodotus, Pindar, or Æschylus, could have read, are in the power of almost every man, in a country where almost every man is instructed to read and write ; and how restless, how difficultly hidden, the powers of genius are ; and yet find even 10 in situations the most favourable, according to Mr. Wordsworth, for the formation of a pure and poetic language,—in situations which ensure familiarity with the grandest objects of the imagination,—but *one* BURNS, among the shepherds of *Scotland*, and not a single poet of humble life among those of *English* lakes and mountains ; I conclude, that POETIC GENIUS is not only a very delicate but a very rare plant.

But be this as it may, the feelings with which

> I think of CHATTERTON, the marvellous boy,   20
> The sleepless soul, that perished in his pride ;
> Of BURNS, that walk'd in glory and in joy
> Behind his plough upon the mountain-side—

are widely different from those with which I should read a *poem*, where the author, having occasion for the character of a poet and a philosopher in the fable of his narration, had chosen to make him a *chimney-sweeper* ; and then, in order to remove all doubts on the subject, had *invented* an account of his birth, parentage, and education, with all the strange and fortunate accidents which had concurred 30 in making him at once poet, philosopher, and sweep ! Nothing but biography can justify this. If it be admissible even in a *Novel*, it must be one in the manner of De Foe's, that were meant to pass for histories, not in the manner of Fielding's : in the life of Moll Flanders, or Colonel Jack, not in a Tom Jones, or even a Joseph Andrews. Much less then can it be legitimately introduced in a *poem*, the characters of which, amid the strongest individualization, must still remain representative. The precepts of Horace, on this point, are grounded on the nature both of poetry and of the human mind. They are not more peremptory, than wise and prudent. For in the first place a deviation from them perplexes the reader's feelings, and all the circumstances, which are feigned in order to make such accidents less improbable, divide and disquiet his faith, rather than aid and support it. Spite of all attempts, the fiction *will* appear, and unfortunately not as *fictitious* but as *false*. The reader not only *knows* that the sentiments and language are the poet's own, and his own too in his *artificial* character, *as poet* ; but by the fruitless endeavours to make him think the contrary, he is not even suffered to *forget* it. . . .

Third ; an undue predilection for the *dramatic* form in certain poems, from which one or other of two evils result. Either the thoughts and diction are different from that of the poet, and then there arises an incongruity of style ; or they are the same and indistinguishable, and then it presents a species of ventriloquism, where two are represented as talking, while in truth one man only speaks.

The fourth class of defects is closely connected with the former ; but yet are such as arise likewise from an intensity of feeling disproportionate to *such* knowledge and value of the objects described, as can be fairly anticipated of men in general, even of the most cultivated classes ; and with which therefore few only, and those few particularly circumstanced, can be supposed to sympathize. In this class, I comprise occasional prolixity, repetition, and an eddying, instead of progression, of thought.

Fifth and last ; thoughts and images too great for the subject. This is an approximation to what might be called *mental* bombast, as distinguished from verbal : for, as in the latter there is a disproportion of the expressions to the thoughts, so in this there is a disproportion of thought to the circumstance and occasion. This, by the bye, is a fault of which none but a man of genius is capable. It is the awkwardness and strength of Hercules with the distaff of Omphale.

It is a well-known fact, that bright colours in motion both make and leave the strongest impressions on the eye. Nothing is more likely too, than that a vivid image or visual spectrum, thus originated, may become the link of associa- 10 tion in recalling the feelings and images that had accompanied the original impression. But if we describe this in such lines, as

> They flash upon that inward eye,
> Which is the bliss of solitude !

in what words shall we describe the joy of retrospection, when the images and virtuous actions of a whole well-spent life pass before that conscience which is indeed the *inward* eye : which is indeed ' *the bliss of solitude* ' ? Assuredly we seem to sink most abruptly, not to say burlesquely, and 20 almost as in a *medley*, from this couplet to—

> And then my heart with pleasure fills,
> And dances with the *daffodils*.

[A second instance of this defect is given from *Gipsies*.]

The last instance of this defect (for I know no other than these already cited) is from the Ode, where, speaking of a child, ' a six years' darling of a pigmy size,' he thus addresses him :

Thou best philosopher, who yet dost keep
Thy heritage ! Thou eye among the blind,
That, deaf and silent, read'st the eternal deep,   30
Haunted for ever by the Eternal Mind,—
Mighty Prophet ! Seer blest !
On whom those truths do rest,

Which we are toiling all our lives to find !
Thou, over whom thy immortality
Broods like the day, a master o'er a slave,
A presence that is not to be put by !

Now here, not to stop at the daring spirit of metaphor
which connects the epithets ' deaf and silent ' with the
apostrophized *eye* : or (if we are to refer it to the preceding
word, philosopher) the faulty and equivocal syntax of the
passage ; and without examining the propriety of making
a ' master *brood* o'er a slave ', or the *day* brood *at all*; we
will merely ask, what does all this mean ? In what sense is
a child of that age a *philosopher* ? In what sense does he
read ' the eternal deep ' ? In what sense is he declared to
be ' *for ever haunted* ' by the Supreme Being ? or so inspired
as to deserve the splendid titles of a *mighty prophet*, a
blessed seer ? By reflection ? by knowledge ? by conscious
intuition ? or by *any* form or modification of consciousness ?
These would be tidings indeed ; but such as would pre-
suppose an immediate revelation to the inspired communi-
cator, and require miracles to authenticate his inspiration.
Children at this age give us no such information of themselves ; and at what time were we dipped in the Lethe, which
has produced such utter oblivion of a state so godlike?
There are many of us that still possess some remembrances,
more or less distinct, respecting themselves at six years old ;
pity that the worthless straws only should float, while
treasures, compared with which all the mines of Golconda
and Mexico were but straws, should be absorbed by some
unknown gulf into some unknown abyss. . . .

In what sense can the magnificent attributes, above
quoted, be appropriated to a *child*, which would not make
them equally suitable to a *bee*, or a *dog*, or a *field of corn* :
or even to a ship, or to the wind and waves that propel it ?
The omnipresent Spirit works equally in them, as in the
child ; and the child is equally unconscious of it as they.

It cannot surely be, that the four lines, immediately following, are to contain the explanation?

> To whom the grave
> Is but a lonely bed without the sense or sight
> Of day or the warm light,
> A place of thought where we in waiting lie.

Surely, it cannot be that this wonder-rousing apostrophe is but a comment on the little poem, ' We are seven ' ? that the whole meaning of the passage is reducible to the assertion, that a *child*, who by the bye at six years old would have been better instructed in most Christian families, has no other notion of death than that of lying in a dark, cold place? And still, I hope, not as in a *place of thought !* not the frightful notion of lying *awake* in his grave! The analogy between death and sleep is too simple, too natural, to render so horrid a belief possible for children; even had they not been in the habit, as all Christian children are, of hearing the latter term used to express the former. But if the child's belief be only that ' he is not dead, but sleepeth ', wherein does it differ from that of his father and mother, or any other adult and instructed person? To form an idea of a thing's becoming nothing, or of nothing becoming a thing, is impossible to all finite beings alike, of whatever age, and however educated or uneducated. Thus it is with splendid paradoxes in general. If the words are taken in the common sense, they convey an absurdity; and if, in contempt of dictionaries and custom, they are so interpreted as to avoid the absurdity, the meaning dwindles into some bald truism. Thus you must at once understand the words *contrary* to their common import, in order to arrive at any *sense*; and *according* to their common import, if you are to receive from them any feeling of *sublimity* or *admiration*.

Though the instances of this defect in Mr. Wordsworth's poems are so few, that for themselves it would have been scarce just to attract the reader's attention toward them;

yet I have dwelt on it, and perhaps the more for this very
reason. For being so very few, they cannot sensibly detract
from the reputation of an author who is even characterized
by the number of profound truths in his writings, which will
stand the severest analysis ; and yet few as they are, they
are exactly those passages which his *blind* admirers would be
most likely, and best able, to imitate. But WORDSWORTH,
where he is indeed Wordsworth, may be mimicked by
Copyists, he may be plundered by Plagiarists ; but he can
10 not be imitated, except by those who are not born to be
imitators. For without his depth of feeling and his imaginative power his *sense* would want its vital warmth and
peculiarity ; and without his strong sense, his *mysticism*
would become *sickly*—mere fog, and dimness !

To these defects which, as appears by the extracts, are
only occasional, I may oppose, with far less fear of encoun-
tering the dissent of any candid and intelligent reader, the
following (for the most part correspondent) excellences.
First, an austere purity of language both grammatically
20 and logically ; in short a perfect appropriateness of the
words to the meaning. . . . I am far however from denying
that we have poets whose *general* style possesses the same
excellence, as Mr. Moore, Lord Byron, Mr. Bowles, and, in
all his later and more important works, our laurel-honouring
Laureate. But there are none, in whose works I do not
appear to myself to find *more* exceptions than in those of
Wordsworth. Quotations or specimens would here be
wholly out of place, and must be left for the critic who
doubts and would invalidate the justice of this eulogy so
30 applied.

The second characteristic excellence of Mr. W's work is :
a correspondent weight and sanity of the Thoughts and
Sentiments, won—not from books, but—from the poet's
own meditative observation. They are *fresh* and have
the dew upon them. His muse, at least when in her

strength of wing, and when she hovers aloft in her proper element,

> Makes audible a linked lay of truth,
> Of truth profound a sweet continuous lay,
> Not learnt, but native, her own natural notes!
> S. T. C.

Even throughout his smaller poems there is scarcely one which is not rendered valuable by some just and original reflection.

See the two following passages in one of his humblest compositions:

> O Reader! had you in your mind
> Such stores as silent thought can bring,
> O gentle Reader! you would find
> A tale in every thing;

and

> I've heard of hearts unkind, kind deeds
> With coldness still returning;
> Alas! the gratitude of men
> Has oftener left me mourning;

or in a still higher strain the six beautiful quatrains,

> Thus fares it still in our decay:
> And yet the wiser mind
> Mourns less for what age takes away
> Than what it leaves behind.
>
> The Blackbird in the summer trees,
> The Lark upon the hill,
> Let loose their carols when they please,
> Are quiet when they will.
>
> With nature never do *they* wage
> A foolish strife; they see
> A happy youth, and their old age
> Is beautiful and free!
>
> But we are pressed by heavy laws;
> And often, glad no more,
> We wear a face of joy, because
> We have been glad of yore.

If there is one who need bemoan
His kindred laid in earth,
The household hearts that were his own,
It is the man of mirth.

My days, my Friend, are almost gone,
My life has been approved,
And many love me ; but by none
Am I enough beloved ;

or the sonnet on Buonaparte ; or finally (for a volume
10 would scarce suffice to exhaust the instances) the last
stanza of the poem on the withered Celandine :

To be a prodigal's favourite—then, worse truth,
A miser's pensioner—behold our lot !
O man ! that from thy fair and shining youth
Age might but take the things youth needed not.

Both in respect of this and of the former excellence,
Mr. Wordsworth strikingly resembles Samuel Daniel, one of
the golden writers of our golden Elizabethan age, now most
causelessly neglected : Samuel Daniel, whose diction bears
20 no mark of time, no distinction of age, which has been, and
as long as our language shall last, will be so far the language
of the to-day and for ever, as that it is more intelligible to
us, than the transitory fashions of our own particular age.
A similar praise is due to his sentiments. No frequency of
perusal can deprive them of their freshness. For though
they are brought into the full day-light of every reader's
comprehension, yet are they drawn up from depths which
few in any age are priviledged to visit, into which few
in any age have courage or inclination to descend. If
30 Mr. Wordsworth is not equally with Daniel alike intelligible
to all readers of average understanding in all passages of his
works, the comparative difficulty does not arise from the
greater impurity of the ore, but from the nature and uses
of the metal. A poem is not necessarily obscure, because

it does not aim to be popular. It is enough, if a work be perspicuous to those for whom it is written, and

> Fit audience find, though few.

To the ' Ode on the intimations of immortality from recollections of early childhood ' the poet might have prefixed the lines which Dante addresses to one of his own Canzoni—

> Canzon, io credo, che saranno radi
> Che tua ragione intendan bene,
> Tanto lor sei faticoso ed alto.

> O lyric song, there will be few, think I,
> Who may thy import understand aright :
> Thou art for *them* so arduous and so high !

10

But the ode was intended for such readers only as had been accustomed to watch the flux and reflux of their inmost nature, to venture at times into the twilight realms of consciousness, and to feel a deep interest in modes of inmost being, to which they know that the attributes of time and space are inapplicable and alien, but which yet can not be conveyed save in symbols of time and space. For such readers the sense is sufficiently plain, and they will be as 20 little disposed to charge Mr. Wordsworth with believing the Platonic pre-existence in the ordinary interpretation of the words, as I am to believe, that Plato himself ever meant or taught it.

Third (and wherein he soars far above Daniel) the sinewy strength and originality of single lines and paragraphs : the frequent *curiosa felicitas* of his diction, of which I need not here give specimens, having anticipated them in a preceding page. This beauty, and as eminently characteristic of Wordsworth's poetry, his rudest assailants have felt them- 30 selves compelled to acknowledge and admire.

Fourth ; the perfect truth of nature in his images and descriptions, as taken immediately from nature, and proving

a long and genial intimacy with the very spirit which gives
the physiognomic expression to all the works of nature. Like
a green field reflected in a calm and perfectly transparent
lake, the image is distinguished from the reality only by its
greater softness and lustre. Like the moisture or the polish
on a pebble, genius neither distorts nor false-colours its
objects ; but on the contrary brings out many a vein and
many a tint, which escapes the eye of common observation,
thus raising to the rank of gems what had been often kicked
10 away by the hurrying foot of the traveller on the dusty high
road of custom.

Let me refer to the whole description of skating, especially
to the lines

> So through the darkness and the cold we flew,
> And not a voice was idle : with the din
> Meanwhile the precipices rang aloud ;
> The leafless trees and every icy crag
> Tinkled like iron ; while the distant hills
> Into the tumult sent an alien sound
> 20 Of melancholy, not unnoticed, while the stars
> Eastward were sparkling clear, and in the west
> The orange sky of evening died away.

Or to the poem on the green linnet. What can be more
accurate yet more lovely than the two concluding stanzas ?

> Upon yon tuft of hazel trees,
> That twinkle to the gusty breeze,
> Behold him perched in ecstasies,
>   Yet seeming still to hover ;
> There ! where the flutter of his wings
> 30 Upon his back and body flings
> Shadows and sunny glimmerings
>   That cover him all over.
>
> While thus before my eyes he gleams
> A brother of the leaves he seems ;
> When in a moment forth he teems
>   His little song in gushes :

As if it pleased him to disdain
And mock the form which he did feign
While he was dancing with the train
Of leaves among the bushes.

Or the description of the blue-cap, and of the noon-tide
silence; or the poem to the cuckoo; or, lastly, though
I might multiply the references to ten times the number,
to the poem, so completely Wordsworth's, commencing

Three years she grew in sun and shower, &c.

Fifth: a meditative pathos, a union of deep and subtle 10
thought with sensibility; a sympathy with man as man;
the sympathy indeed of a contemplator, rather than a
fellow-sufferer or co-mate (*spectator, haud particeps*) but
of a contemplator, from whose view no difference of rank
conceals the sameness of the nature; no injuries of wind
or weather, or toil, or even of ignorance, wholly disguise the
human face divine. The superscription and the image of
the Creator still remain legible to *him* under the dark lines,
with which guilt or calamity had cancelled or cross-barred
it. Here the man and the poet lose and find themselves in 20
each other, the one as glorified, the latter as substantiated.
In this mild and philosophic pathos, Wordsworth appears
to me without a compeer. Such he *is*: so he *writes*. . . .
Last, and pre-eminently, I challenge for this poet the gift
of IMAGINATION in the highest and strictest sense of the
word. In the play of *Fancy*, Wordsworth, to my feelings,
is not always graceful, and sometimes *recondite*. The *like-
ness* is occasionally too strange, or demands too peculiar
a point of view, or is such as appears the creature of pre-
determined research, rather than spontaneous presentation. 30
Indeed his fancy seldom displays itself as mere and unmodi-
fied fancy. But in imaginative power, he stands nearest
of all modern writers to Shakespeare and Milton; and yet
in a kind perfectly unborrowed and his own. To employ

his own words, which are at once an instance and an illustration, he does indeed to all thoughts and to all objects

> ————————————add the gleam,
> The light that never was, on sea or land,
> The consecration, and the poet's dream.

I shall select a few examples as most obviously manifesting this faculty ; but if I should ever be fortunate enough to render my analysis of imagination, its origin and characters, thoroughly intelligible to the reader, he will scarcely
10 open on a page of this poet's works without recognising, more or less, the presence and the influences of this faculty.

From the poem on the Yew Trees,

> But worthier still of note
> Are those fraternal four of Borrowdale,
> Joined in one solemn and capacious grove :
> Huge trunks !—and each particular trunk a growth
> Of intertwisted fibres serpentine
> Up-coiling, and inveterately convolved—
> Not uninformed with phantasy, and looks
20 That threaten the profane ;—a pillared shade,
> Upon whose grassless floor of red-brown hue,
> By sheddings from the pinal umbrage tinged
> Perennially—beneath whose sable roof
> Of boughs, as if for festal purpose decked
> With unrejoicing berries, ghostly shapes
> May meet at noontide—FEAR and trembling HOPE,
> SILENCE and FORESIGHT—DEATH, the skeleton,
> And TIME, the shadow—there to celebrate,
> As in a natural temple scattered o'er
30 With altars undisturbed of mossy stone,
> United worship ; or in mute repose
> To lie, and listen to the mountain flood
> Murmuring from Glaramara's inmost caves.

The effect of the old man's figure in the poem of Resolution and Independence.

> While he was talking thus, the lonely place,
> The old man's shape, and speech, all troubled me :

In my mind's eye I seemed to see him pace
About the weary moors continually,
Wandering about alone and silently.

Or the 8th, 9th, 19th, 26th, 31st, and 33d, in the collection of miscellaneous sonnets—the sonnet on the subjugation of Switzerland, or the last ode.

[The two stanzas or paragraphs in the *Intimations of Immortality* beginning ' Our birth is but a sleep and a forgetting ' and ' O joy that in our embers ' are selected for quotation, and are followed by a passage from *The White Doe of Rylstone*.]

The following analogy will, I am apprehensive, appear dim and fantastic, but in reading Bartram's Travels I could not help transcribing the following lines as a sort of allegory or connected simile and metaphor of Wordsworth's intellect and genius.—' The soil is a deep, rich, dark mould, on a deep stratum of tenacious clay ; and that on a foundation of rocks, which often break through both strata, lifting their back above the surface. The trees which chiefly grow here are the gigantic black oak ; magnolia magni-floria ; fraximus excelsior ; platane ; and a few stately tulip trees.' What Mr. Wordsworth *will* produce, it is not for me to prophecy : but I could pronounce with the liveliest convictions what he is capable of producing. It is the FIRST GENUINE PHILOSOPHIC POEM.

The preceding criticism will not, I am aware, avail to overcome the prejudices of those who have made it a business to attack and ridicule Mr. Wordsworth's compositions. . . . On the other hand, much as I might wish for their fuller sympathy, I dare not flatter myself, that the freedom with which I have declared my opinions concerning both his theory and his defects, most of which are more or less connected with his theory, either as cause or effect, will be satisfactory or pleasing to *all* the poet's admirers and advocates. More indiscriminate than mine their admiration may

be : deeper and more sincere it can not be. But I have
advanced no opinion either for praise or censure, other than
as texts introductory to the reasons which compel me to
form it. Above all, I was fully convinced that such a criticism was not only wanted, but that, if executed with ade-
quate ability, it must conduce, in no mean degree, to Mr.
Wordsworth's *reputation*. His *fame* belongs to another age,
and can neither be accelerated nor retarded. How small
the proportion of the defects are to the beauties, I have
10 repeatedly declared ; and that no one of them originates in
deficiency of poetic genius. Had they been more and greater,
I should still, as a friend to his literary character in the
present age, consider an analytic display of them as *pure
gain* ; if only it removed, as surely to all reflecting minds
even the foregoing analysis must have removed, the strange
mistake, so slightly grounded, yet so widely and industriously propagated, of Mr. Wordsworth's turn for SIMPLICITY !
I am not half so much irritated by hearing his enemies abuse
him for vulgarity of style, subject, and conception, as I am
20 disgusted with the gilded side of the same meaning, as displayed by some affected admirers, with whom he is, forsooth,
a *sweet, simple poet !* and *so* natural, that little master
Charles and his younger sister are *so* charmed with them,
that they play at ' Goody Blake ', or at ' Johnny and Betty
Foy ! '

From HAZLITT'S

SPIRIT OF THE AGE

MR. WORDSWORTH'S genius is a pure emanation of the
Spirit of the Age. Had he lived in any other period of the
world, he would never have been heard of. As it is, he has
some difficulty to contend with the hebetude of his intellect
and the meanness of his subject. With him ' lowliness is
young ambition's ladder ' : but he finds it a toil to climb in
this way the steep of Fame. His homely Muse can hardly
raise her wing from the ground, nor spread her hidden
glories to the sun. He has ' no figures nor no fantasies,
which busy *passion* draws in the brains of men ' : neither 10
the gorgeous machinery of mythologic lore, nor the splendid colours of poetic diction. His style is vernacular : he
delivers household truths. He sees nothing loftier than
human hopes, nothing deeper than the human heart. This
he probes, this he tampers with, this he poises, with all its
incalculable weight of thought and feeling, in his hands, and
at the same time calms the throbbing pulses of his own
heart by keeping his eye ever fixed on the face of nature.
If he can make the life-blood flow from the wounded breast,
this is the living colouring with which he paints his verse : 20
if he can assuage the pain or close up the wound with the
balm of solitary musing, or the healing power of plants and
herbs and ' skyey influences ', this is the sole triumph of
his art. He takes the simplest elements of nature and of
the human mind, the mere abstract conditions inseparable
from our being, and tries to compound a new system of
poetry from them ; and has perhaps succeeded as well as
any one could. ' *Nihil humani a me alienum puto* ' is the
motto of his works. He thinks nothing low or indifferent of
which this can be affirmed : every thing that professes to be 30

more than this, that is not an absolute essence of truth and feeling, he holds to be vitiated, false and spurious. In a word, his poetry is founded on setting up an opposition (and pushing it to the utmost length) between the natural and the artificial, between the spirit of humanity and the spirit of fashion and of the world.

It is one of the innovations of the time. It partakes of, and is carried along with, the revolutionary movement of our age : the political changes of the day were the model 10 on which he formed and conducted his poetical experiments. His Muse (it cannot be denied, and without this we cannot explain its character at all) is a levelling one. It proceeds on a principle of equality, and strives to reduce all things to the same standard. It is distinguished by a proud humility. It relies upon its own resources, and disdains external show and relief. It takes the commonest events and objects, as a test to prove that nature is always interesting from its inherent truth and beauty, without any of the ornaments of dress or pomp of circumstances to set it off. 20 Hence the unaccountable mixture of seeming simplicity and real abstruseness in the *Lyrical Ballads*. Fools have laughed at, wise men scarcely understand, them. He takes a subject or a story merely as pegs or loops to hang thought and feeling on; the incidents are trifling, in proportion to his contempt for imposing appearances ; the reflections are profound, according to the gravity and aspiring pretensions of his mind.

His popular, inartificial style gets rid (at a blow) of all the trappings of verse, of all the high places of poetry : 30 ' the cloud-capt towers, the solemn temples, the gorgeous palaces,' are swept to the ground, and ' like the baseless fabric of a vision, leave not a wreck behind '. All the traditions of learning, all the superstitions of age, are obliterated and effaced. We begin *de novo* on a *tabula rasa* of poetry. The purple pall, the nodding plume of tragedy are exploded as mere pantomime and trick, to return to the simplicity of truth and nature. Kings, queens, priests, nobles, the altar and the throne, the distinctions of rank, birth, wealth, power, ' the judge's robe, the marshal's truncheon, the ceremony that to great ones 'longs,' are not to be found here. The author tramples on the pride of art with greater pride. The Ode and Epode, the Strophe and the Antistrophe, he laughs to scorn. The harp of Homer, the trump of Pindar and of Alcæus, are still. The decencies of costume, the decorations of vanity are stripped off without 10 mercy as barbarous, idle, and Gothic. The jewels in the crisped hair, the diadem on the polished brow, are thought meretricious, theatrical, vulgar ; and nothing contents his fastidious taste beyond a simple garland of flowers. Neither does he avail himself of the advantages which nature or accident holds out to him. He chooses to have his subject a foil to his invention, to owe nothing but to himself.

He gathers manna in the wilderness ; he strikes the barren rock for the gushing moisture. He elevates the mean by the strength of his own aspirations ; he clothes the naked 20 with beauty and grandeur from the stories of his own re-collections. No cypress grove loads his verse with funeral pomp : but his imagination lends ' a sense of joy

> To the bare trees and mountains bare,
> And grass in the green field.'

No storm, no shipwreck startles us by its horrors : but the rainbow lifts its head in the cloud, and the breeze sighs through the withered fern. No sad vicissitude of fate, no overwhelming catastrophe in nature deforms his page : but the dew-drop glitters on the bending flower, the tear collects 30 in the glistening eye.

> Beneath the hills, along the flowery vales,
> The generations are prepared ; the pangs,
> The internal pangs are ready ; the dread strife
> Of poor humanity's afflicted will,
> Struggling in vain with ruthless destiny.

As the lark ascends from its low bed on fluttering wing, and salutes the morning skies, so Mr. Wordsworth's unpretending Muse in russet guise scales the summits of reflection, while it makes the round earth its footstool and its home !

Possibly a good deal of this may be regarded as the effect of disappointed views and an inverted ambition. Prevented by native pride and indolence from climbing the ascent of learning or greatness, taught by political opinions to say to the vain pomp and glory of the world, ' I hate ye,' seeing
10 the path of classical and artificial poetry blocked up by the cumbrous ornaments of style and turgid *common-places*, so that nothing more could be achieved in that direction but by the most ridiculous bombast or the tamest servility, he has turned back, partly from the bias of his mind, partly perhaps from a judicious policy—has struck into the sequestered vale of humble life, sought out the Muse among sheep-cotes and hamlets, and the peasant's mountain-haunts, has discarded all the tinsel pageantry of verse, and endeavoured (not in vain) to aggrandise the trivial, and add the
20 charm of novelty to the familiar. No one has shown the same imagination in raising trifles into importance : no one has displayed the same pathos in treating of the simplest feelings of the heart. Reserved, yet haughty, having no unruly or violent passions (or those passions having been early suppressed), Mr. Wordsworth has passed his life in solitary musing or in daily converse with the face of nature. He exemplifies in an eminent degree the *association* ; for his poetry has no other source or character. He has dwelt among pastoral scenes, till each object has become con-
30 nected with a thousand feelings, a link in the chain of thought, a fibre of his own heart. Every one is by habit and familiarity strongly attached to the place of his birth, or to objects that recall the most pleasing and eventful circumstances of his life.

But to the author of the *Lyrical Ballads* nature is a kind

of home ; and he may be said to take a personal interest
in the universe. There is no image so insignificant that it
has not in some mood or other found the way into his heart :
no sound that does not awaken the memory of other years.—

> To him the meanest flower that blows can give
> Thoughts that do often lie too deep for tears.

The daisy looks up to him with sparkling eye as an old
acquaintance : the cuckoo haunts him with sounds of early
youth not to be expressed : a linnet's nest startles him with
boyish delight : an old withered thorn is weighed down
with a heap of recollections : a grey cloak, seen on some
wild moor, torn by the wind or drenched in the rain, after-
wards becomes an object of imagination to him : even the
lichens on the rock have a life and being in his thoughts.
He has described all these objects in a way and with an
intensity of feeling that no one else had done before him,
and has given a new view or aspect of nature. He is in this
sense the most original poet now living, and the one whose
writings could the least be spared : for they have no substitute elsewhere. The vulgar do not read them ; the learned,
who see all things through books, do not understand them ;
the great despise. The fashionable may ridicule them ; but
the author has created himself an interest in the heart
of the retired and lonely student of nature, which can
never die.

Persons of this class will still continue to feel what he has
felt : he has expressed what they might in vain wish to
express, except with glistening eye and faltering tongue !
There is a lofty philosophic tone, a thoughtful humanity,
infused into his pastoral vein. Remote from the passions
and events of the great world, he has communicated interest
and dignity to the primal movements of the heart of man,
and ingrafted his own conscious reflections on the casual
thoughts of hinds and shepherds. Nursed amidst the

grandeur of mountain scenery, he has stooped to have
a nearer view of the daisy under his feet, or plucked a branch
of white-thorn from its spray : but, in describing it, his
mind seems imbued with the majesty and solemnity of the
objects around him. The tall rock lifts its head in the erect-
ness of his spirit ; the cataract roars in the sound of his
verse ; and in its dim and mysterious meaning the mists
seem to gather in the hollows of Helvellyn, and the forked
Skiddaw hovers in the distance. There is little mention of
10 mountainous scenery in Mr. Wordsworth's poetry ; but by
internal evidence one might be almost sure that it was
written in a mountainous country, from its bareness, its
simplicity, its loftiness and its depth !

His later philosophic productions have a somewhat
different character. They are a departure from, a dere-
liction of, his first principles. They are classical and
courtly. They are polished in style without being gaudy,
dignified in subject without affectation. They seem to have
been composed not in a cottage at Grasmere, but among the
20 half-inspired groves and stately recollections of Cole-Orton.
We might allude in particular, for examples of what we
mean, to the lines on a Picture by Claude Lorraine and to
the exquisite poem, entitled *Laodamia*. The last of these
breathes the pure spirit of the finest fragments of antiquity—
the sweetness, the gravity, the strength, the beauty and the
languor of death—

Calm contemplation and majestic pains.

Its glossy brilliancy arises from the perfection of the finish-
ing, like that of a careful sculpture, not from gaudy colour-
30 ing. The texture of the thoughts has the smoothness and
solidity of marble. It is a poem that might be read aloud
in Elysium, and the spirits of departed heroes and sages
would gather round to listen to it !

Mr. Wordsworth's philosophic poetry, with a less glowing

aspect and less tumult in the veins than Lord Byron's on
similar occasions, bends a calmer and keener eye on mortality ; the impression, if less vivid, is more pleasing and
permanent ; and we confess it (perhaps it is a want of taste
and proper feeling) that there are lines and poems of our
author's, that we think of ten times for once that we recur
to any of Lord Byron's. Or if there are any of the latter's
writings that we can dwell upon in the same way, that is,
as lasting and heart-felt sentiments, it is when laying aside
his usual pomp and pretension, he descends with Mr. Words- 10
worth to the common ground of a disinterested humanity.
It may be considered as characteristic of our poet's writings,
that they either make no impression on the mind at all, seem
mere *nonsense-verses*, or that they leave a mark behind them
that never wears out. They either

Fall blunted from the indurated breast—

without any perceptible result, or they absorb it like a
passion. To one class of readers he appears sublime, to
another (and we fear the largest) ridiculous. He has probably realised Milton's wish,—' and fit audience found, 20
though few : ' but we suspect he is not reconciled to the
alternative.

There are delightful passages in the EXCURSION, both of
natural description and of inspired reflection (passages of
the latter kind that in the sound of the thoughts and of the
swelling language resemble heavenly symphonies, mournful
requiems over the grave of human hopes) ; but we must add,
in justice and in sincerity, that we think it impossible that
this work should ever become popular, even in the same
degree as the *Lyrical Ballads.* It affects a system without 30
having any intelligible clue to one, and, instead of unfolding
a principle in various and striking lights, repeats the same
conclusions till they become flat and insipid. Mr. Wordsworth's mind is obtuse, except as it is the organ and the

receptacle of accumulated feelings : it is not analytic, but
synthetic ; it is reflecting, rather than theoretical.   The
EXCURSION, we believe, fell still-born from the press.   There
was something abortive, and clumsy, and ill-judged in the
attempt.   It was long and laboured.   The personages, for
the most part, were low, the fare rustic ; the plan raised
expectations which were not fulfilled ; and the effect was
like being ushered into a stately hall and invited to sit down
to a splendid banquet in the company of clowns, and with
10 nothing but successive courses of apple-dumplings served
up.   It was not even *toujours perdrix* !

Mr. Wordsworth, in his person, is above the middle size,
with marked features and an air somewhat stately and
quixotic.   He reminds one of some of Holbein's heads :
grave, saturnine, with a slight indication of sly humour, kept
under by the manners of the age or by the pretensions of
the person.   He has a peculiar sweetness in his smile, and
great depth and manliness and a rugged harmony in the
tones of his voice.   His manner of reading his own poetry
20 is particularly imposing ; and in his favourite passages his
eye beams with preternatural lustre, and the meaning
labours slowly up from his swelling breast.   No one who has
seen him at these moments could go away with an impression
that he was a ' man of no mark or likelihood '.   Perhaps
the comment of his face and voice is necessary to convey
a full idea of his poetry.   His language may not be intelligible ; but his manner is not to be mistaken.   It is clear that
he is either mad or inspired.   In company, even in a *tête-à-
tête*, Mr. Wordsworth is often silent, indolent and reserved.
30 If he is become verbose and oracular of late years, he was
not so in his better days.   He threw out a bold or an indifferent remark without either effort or pretension, and
relapsed into musing again.   He shone most (because he
seemed most roused and animated) in reciting his own
poetry, or in talking about it.   He sometimes gave striking

views of his feelings and trains of association in composing
certain passages ; or if one did not always understand his
distinctions, still there was no want of interest : there was
a latent meaning worth inquiring into, like a vein of ore that
one cannot exactly hit upon at the moment, but of which
there are sure indications. His standard of poetry is high
and severe, almost to exclusiveness. He admits of nothing
below, scarcely of anything above, himself. It is fine to hear
him talk of the way in which certain subjects should have
been treated by eminent poets, according to his notions of 10
the art. Thus he finds fault with Dryden's description of
Bacchus in the *Alexander's Feast*, as if he were a mere good-
looking youth or boon companion—

> Flushed with a purple grace,
> He shows his honest face—

instead of representing the God returning from the conquest
of India, crowned with vine-leaves and drawn by panthers,
and followed by troops of satyrs, of wild men and animals
that he had tamed. You would think, in hearing him speak
on this subject, that you saw Titian's picture of the meeting 20
of *Bacchus and Ariadne*—so classic were his conceptions, so
glowing his style.

Milton is his great idol, and he sometimes dares to compare himself with him. His Sonnets, indeed, have something
of the same high-raised tone and prophetic spirit. Chaucer
is another prime favourite of his, and he has been at the
pains to modernize some of the *Canterbury Tales*. Those
persons, who look upon Mr. Wordsworth as a merely puerile
writer, must be rather at a loss to account for his strong
predilection for such geniuses as Dante and Michael Angelo. 30
We do not think our author has any very cordial sympathy
with Shakespeare. How should he ? Shakespeare was the
least of an egotist of any body in the world. He does not
much relish the variety and scope of dramatic composition.

' He hates those interlocutions between Lucius and Caius.'
Yet Mr. Wordsworth himself wrote a tragedy when he was
young ; and we have heard the following energetic lines
quoted from it, as put into the mouth of a person smit with
remorse for some rash crime :

> ——Action is momentary,
> The motion of a muscle this way or that ;
> Suffering is long, obscure and infinite !

Perhaps for want of light and shade, and the unshackled
spirit of the drama, this performance was never brought
forward. Our critic has a great dislike to Gray, and a fondness for Thomson and Collins. It is mortifying to hear him
speak of Pope and Dryden whom, because they have been
supposed to have all the possible excellences of poetry, he
will allow to have none.

Nothing, however, can be fairer, or more amusing than the
way in which he sometimes exposes the unmeaning verbiage
of modern poetry. Thus, in the beginning of Dr. Johnson's *Vanity of Human Wishes*—

> Let observation with extensive view
> Survey mankind from China to Peru—

he says there is a total want of imagination accompanying
the words ; the same idea is repeated three times under the
disguise of a different phraseology. It comes to this : ' let
observation with extensive *observation observe* mankind ' ; or
take away the first line, and the second,

> Survey mankind from China to Peru,

literally conveys the whole. Mr. Wordsworth is, we must
say, a perfect Drawcansir as to prose writers. He complains
of the dry reasoners and matter-of-fact people for their want
of *passion* ; and he is jealous of the rhetorical declaimers
and rhapsodists as trenching on the province of poetry. He
condemns all French writers (as well of poetry as prose) in

the lump. His list in this way is indeed small. He approves of Walton's *Angler*, Paley, and some other writers of an inoffensive modesty of pretension. He also likes books of voyages and travels, and *Robinson Crusoe*. In art, he greatly esteems Bewick's woodcuts and Waterloo's sylvan etchings. But he sometimes takes a higher tone, and gives his mind fair play. We have known him enlarge with a noble intelligence and enthusiasm on Nicolas Poussin's fine landscape-compositions, pointing out the unity of design that pervades them, the superintending mind, the imagina- 10 tive principle that brings all to bear on the same end ; and declaring he would not give a rush for any landscape that did not express the time of day, the climate, the period of the world it was meant to illustrate, or had not this character of *wholeness* in it.

His eye also does justice to Rembrandt's fine and masterly effects. In the way in which that artist works something out of nothing, and transforms the stump of a tree, a common figure, into an *ideal* object by the gorgeous light and shade thrown upon it, he perceives an analogy to his 20 own mode of investing the minute details of nature with an atmosphere of sentiment, and in pronouncing Rembrandt to be a man of genius, feels that he strengthens his own claim to the title. It has been said of Mr. Wordsworth, that ' he hates conchology, that he hates the Venus of Medicis '. But these, we hope, are mere epigrams and *jeux-d'esprit*, as far from truth as they are free from malice : a sort of running satire or critical clenches—

> Where one for sense and one for rhyme
> Is quite sufficient at one time. 30

We think, however, that if Mr. Wordsworth had been a more liberal and candid critic, he would have been a more sterling writer. If a greater number of sources of pleasure had been open to him, he would have communicated pleasure to the world more frequently. Had he been less fastidious in pronouncing sentence on the works of others, his own would have been received more favourably, and treated more leniently. The current of his feelings is deep, but narrow ; the range of his understanding is lofty and aspiring rather than discursive. The force, the originality, the absolute truth and identity, with which he feels some things, makes him indifferent to so many others. The simplicity and enthusiasm of his feelings, with respect to nature, render him bigoted and intolerant in his judgments of men and things. But it happens to him, as to others, that his strength lies in his weakness ; and perhaps we have no right to complain. We might get rid of the cynic and the egotist, and find in his stead a common-place man. We should ' take the good the Gods provide us ' : a fine and original vein of poetry is not one of their most contemptible gifts ; and the rest is scarcely worth thinking of, except as it may be a mortification to those who expect perfection from human nature, or who have been idle enough at some period of their lives to deify men of genius as possessing claims above it. But this is a chord that jars, and we shall not dwell upon it.

Lord Byron we have called, according to the old proverb, ' the spoiled child of fortune ' : Mr. Wordsworth might plead, in mitigation of some peculiarities, that he is ' the spoiled child of disappointment '. We are convinced, if he had been early a popular poet, he would have borne his honours meekly, and would have been a person of great *bonhomie* and frankness of disposition. But the sense of injustice and of undeserved ridicule sours the temper and narrows the views. To have produced works of genius, and to find them neglected or treated with scorn, is one of the heaviest trials of human patience. We exaggerate our own merits when they are denied by others, and are apt to grudge and cavil at every particle of praise bestowed on those to whom we feel a conscious superiority. In mere self-defence we turn against the world when it turns against us, brood over the undeserved slights we receive ; and thus the genial current of the soul is stopped, or vents itself in effusions of petulance and self-conceit. Mr. Wordsworth has thought too much of contemporary critics and criticism, and less than he ought of the award of posterity and of the opinion, we do not say of private friends, but of those who were made so by their admiration of his genius.

He did not court popularity by a conformity to estab-lished models, and he ought not to have been surprised that 10 his originality was not understood as a matter of course. He has *gnawed too much on the bridle*, and has often thrown out crusts to the critics, in mere defiance or as a point of honour when he was challenged, which otherwise his own good sense would have withheld. We suspect that Mr. Wordsworth's feelings are a little morbid in this respect, or that he resents censure more than he is gratified by praise. Otherwise, the tide has turned much in his favour of late years. He has a large body of determined partisans, and is at present sufficiently in request with the public to save or 20 relieve him from the last necessity to which a man of genius can be reduced—that of becoming the God of his own idolatry !

. . . .

Not, therefore, in the *Excursion* must we look for that reversionary influence which awaits Wordsworth with posterity. It is the vulgar superstition in behalf of big books and sounding pretensions, that must have prevailed upon Coleridge and others to undervalue, by comparison with the direct philosophic poetry of Wordsworth, those earlier poems which are all short, but generally scintillating with gems of far profounder truth. I speak of that truth which strengthens into solemnity an impression very feebly acknowledged previously, or truth which suddenly unveils a connexion between objects hitherto regarded as irrelate and independent. In astronomy, to gain the rank of discoverer, it is not required that you should reveal a star absolutely new : find out with respect to an old star some new affection—as, for instance, that it has an ascertainable parallax—and immediately you bring it within the verge of a human interest ; or with respect to some old familiar planet, that its satellites suffer periodical eclipses, and immediately you bring it within the verge of terrestrial uses. Gleams of steadier vision, that brighten into certainty appearances else doubtful, or that unfold relations else unsuspected, are not less discoveries of truth than the downright revelations of the telescope, or the absolute conquests of the diving-bell. It is astonishing how large a harvest of new truths would be reaped, simply through the accident of a man's feeling, or being made to feel, more *deeply* than other men. He sees the same objects, neither more nor fewer, but he sees them engraved in lines far stronger and more determinate : and the difference in the strength makes the whole difference between consciousness and sub-consciousness. And in questions of the mere understanding, we see the same fact illustrated : the author who wins notice the most, is not he that perplexes men by truths drawn from fountains of absolute novelty—truths as yet unsunned, and from that cause obscure ; but he that awakens into illuminated consciousness ancient lineaments of truth long slumbering in the mind, although too faint to have extorted attention. Wordsworth has brought many a truth into life 10 both for the eye and for the understanding, which previously had slumbered indistinctly for all men.

For instance, as respects the eye, who does not acknowledge instantaneously the magical strength of truth in his saying of a cataract seen from a station two miles off, that it was ' frozen by distance ' ? In all nature, there is not an object so essentially at war with the stiffening of frost, as the headlong and desperate life of a cataract ; and yet notoriously the effect of distance is to lock up this frenzy of motion into the most petrific column of stillness. This 20 effect is perceived at once when pointed out ; but how few are the eyes that ever *would* have perceived it for themselves ! Twilight, again—who before Wordsworth ever distinctly noticed its *abstracting* power ?—that power of removing, softening, harmonizing, by which a mode of obscurity executes for the eye the same mysterious office which the mind so often, within its own shadowy realms, executes for itself. In the dim interspace between day and night, all disappears from our earthly scenery, as if touched by an enchanter's rod, which is either mean or inharmonious 30 or unquiet, or expressive of temporary things. Leaning against a column of rock, looking down upon a lake or river, and at intervals carrying your eyes forward through a vista of mountains, you become aware that your sight rests upon the very same spectacle, unaltered in a single feature, which

D

once at the same hour was beheld by the legionary Roman from his embattled camp, or by the roving Briton in his ' wolf-skin vest ', lying down to sleep, and looking

> Through some leafy bower,
> Before his eyes were closed.

How magnificent is the summary or abstraction of the elementary features in such a scene, as executed by the poet himself, in illustration of this abstraction daily executed by nature, through her handmaid Twilight ! Listen, reader,
10 to the closing strain, solemn as twilight is solemn, and grand as the spectacle which it describes :—

> By him [i.e. the roving Briton] was seen,
> The self-same vision which *we* now behold,
> At thy meek bidding, shadowy Power, brought forth ;
> These mighty barriers, and the gulf between ;
> The flood, the stars—a spectacle as old
> As the beginning of the heavens and earth.

Another great field there is amongst the pomps of nature, which, if Wordsworth did not first notice, he certainly has
20 noticed most circumstantially. I speak of cloud-scenery, or those pageants of sky-built architecture, which sometimes in summer, at noonday, and in all seasons about sunset, arrest or appal the meditative ; ' perplexing monarchs ' with the spectacle of armies manœuvring, or deepening the solemnity of evening by towering edifices, that mimic—but which also in mimicking mock—the transitory grandeurs of man. It is singular that these gorgeous phenomena, not less than those of the *aurora borealis*, have been so little noticed by poets. The *aurora* was naturally neglected by the
30 southern poets of Greece and Rome, as not much seen in their latitudes. But the cloud-architecture of the daylight belongs alike to north and south. Accordingly, I remember one notice of it in Hesiod, a case where the clouds exhibited

> The beauteous semblance of a flock at rest.

Another there is, a thousand years later, in Lucan : amongst the portents which that poet notices as prefiguring the dreadful convulsions destined to shake the earth at Pharsalia, I remember some fiery coruscation of arms in the heavens ; but, so far as I recollect, the appearances might have belonged equally to the workmanship of the clouds or the *aurora*. Up and down the next eight hundred years, are scattered evanescent allusions to these vapoury appearances; in *Hamlet* and elsewhere occur gleams of such allusions ; but I remember no distinct sketch of such an appearance 10 before that in the *Antony and Cleopatra* of Shakespeare, beginning,

Sometimes we see a cloud that 's dragonish.

Subsequently to Shakespeare, these notices, as of all phenomena whatsoever that demanded a familiarity with nature in the spirit of love, became rarer and rarer. At length, as the eighteenth century was winding up its accounts, forth stepped William Wordsworth, of whom, as a reader of all pages in nature, it may be said that, if we except Dampier, the admirable buccaneer, the gentle 20 *flibustier*, and some few professional naturalists, he first and he last looked at natural objects with the eye that neither will be dazzled from without nor cheated by preconceptions from within. Most men look at nature in the hurry of a confusion that distinguishes nothing ; *their* error is from without. Pope, again, and many who live in towns,[1] make

---

[1] It was not, however, that all poets then lived in towns ; neither had Pope himself generally lived in towns. But it is perfectly useless to be familiar with nature unless there is a public trained to love and value nature. It is not what the individual sees that will fix itself as beautiful in his recollections, but what he sees under a consciousness that others will sympathize with his feelings. Under any other circumstances familiarity does but realize the adage and 'breeds contempt'. The great despisers of rural scenery, its fixed and permanent undervaluers, are rustics.

such blunders as that of supposing the moon to tip with
silver the hills *behind* which she is rising, not by erroneous
use of their eyes (for they use them not at all), but by
inveterate preconceptions. Scarcely has there been a poet
with what could be called a learned eye, or an eye *exten-
sively* learned, before Wordsworth. Much affectation there
has been of that sort since *his* rise, and at all times much
counterfeit enthusiasm ; but the sum of the matter is this,
that Wordsworth had his passion for nature fixed in his
10 blood ; it was a necessity, like that of the mulberry-leaf
to the silkworm ; and through his commerce with nature
did he live and breathe. Hence it was—viz. from the *truth* of
his love—that his knowledge grew ; whilst most others,
being merely hypocrites in their love, have turned out
merely sciolists in their knowledge. This chapter, therefore,
of *sky*-scenery may be said to have been revivified amongst
the resources of poetry by Wordsworth—rekindled, if not
absolutely kindled. The sublime scene indorsed upon the
draperies of the storm in the fourth book of the *Excursion*—
20 that scene again witnessed upon the passage of the Hamilton
Hills in Yorkshire—the solemn ' sky prospect ' from the
fields of France, are unrivalled in that order of composition ;
and in one of these records Wordsworth has given first of all
the true key-note of the sentiment belonging to these grand
pageants. They are, says the poet, speaking in a case where
the appearance had occurred towards night,

> Meek nature's evening comment on the shows
> And all the fuming vanities of earth.

Yes, that is the secret moral whispered to the mind. These
30 mimicries express the laughter which is in heaven at earthly
pomps. Frail and vapoury are the glories of man, even as
the visionary parodies of those glories are frail, even as the
scenical copies of these glories are frail, which nature weaves
in clouds.

As another of those natural appearances which must have haunted men's eyes since the Flood, but yet had never forced itself into *conscious* notice until arrested by Wordsworth, I may notice an effect of *iteration* daily exhibited in the habits of cattle :—

> The cattle are grazing,
> Their heads never raising,
> There are forty feeding like one.

Now, merely as a *fact*, and if it were nothing more, this characteristic appearance in the habits of cows, when all 10 repeat the action of each, ought not to have been overlooked by those who profess themselves engaged in holding up a mirror to nature. But the fact has also a profound meaning as a hieroglyphic. In all animals which live under the protection of man a life of peace and quietness, but do not share in his labours or in his pleasures, what we regard is the species, and not the individual. Nobody but a grazier ever looks at one cow amongst a field of cows, or at one sheep in a flock. But as to those animals which are more closely connected with man, not passively connected, but 20 actively, being partners in his toils, and perils, and recreations—such as horses, dogs, falcons—they are regarded as individuals, and are allowed the benefit of an individual interest. It is not that cows have not a differential character, each for herself ; and sheep, it is well known, have all a separate physiognomy for the shepherd who has cultivated their acquaintance. But men generally have no opportunity or motive for studying the individualities of creatures, however otherwise respectable, that are too much regarded by all of us in the reversionary light of milk, and beef, and 30 mutton. Far otherwise it is with horses, who share in man's martial risks, who sympathize with man's frenzy in hunting, who divide with man the burdens of noonday. Far otherwise it is with dogs, that share the hearths of man, and adore

the footsteps of his children. These man loves ; of these he makes dear, though humble friends. These often fight for *him* ; and for *them* he reciprocally will sometimes fight. Of necessity, therefore, every horse and every dog is an individual—has a sort of personality that makes him *separately* interesting—has a beauty and a character of his own. Go to Melton, therefore, on some crimson morning, and what will you see ? Every man, every horse, every dog, glorying in the plenitude of life, is in a different attitude, motion, ges-
10 ture, action. It is not there the sublime unity which you must seek, where forty are like one ; but the sublime infinity, like that of ocean, like that of Flora, like that of nature, where no repetitions are endured, no leaf is the copy of another leaf, no absolute identity, and no painful tautologies. This subject might be pursued into profounder recesses ; but in a popular discussion it is necessary to forbear.

A volume might be filled with such glimpses of novelty as Wordsworth has first laid bare, even to the apprehension
20 of the *senses*. For the *understanding*, when moving in the same track of human sensibilities, he has done only not so much. How often (to give an instance or two) must the human heart have felt the case, and yearned for an expression of the case, when there are sorrows which descend far below the region in which tears gather; and yet who has ever given utterance to this feeling until Wordsworth came with his immortal line :—

Thoughts that do often lie too deep for tears ?

This sentiment, and others that might be adduced (such
30 as ' The child is father of the man '), have even passed into the popular heart, and are often quoted by those who know not *whom* they are quoting. Magnificent, again, is the sentiment, and yet an echo to one which lurks amongst all hearts, in relation to the frailty of merely human schemes

for working good, which so often droop and collapse through
the unsteadiness of human energies—

> Foundations must be laid
> In heaven.

How ? Foundations laid in realms that are *above* ? But
that is impossible ; *that* is at war with elementary physics ;
foundations must be laid *below*. Yes ; and even so the poet
throws the mind yet more forcibly on the hyperphysical
character—on the grandeur transcending all physics—of
those spiritual and shadowy foundations which alone are 10
enduring.

But the great distinction of Wordsworth, and the pledge
of his increasing popularity, is the extent of his sympathy
with what is *really* permanent in human feelings, and also
the depth of this sympathy. Young and Cowper, the two
earlier leaders in the province of meditative poetry, are too
circumscribed in the range of their sympathies, too narrow,
too illiberal, and too exclusive. Both of these poets manifested the quality of their strength in the quality of their
public reception. Popular in some degree from the first, 20
they entered upon the inheritance of their fame almost at
once. Far different was the fate of Wordsworth ; for in
poetry of this class, which appeals to what lies deepest in man,
in proportion to the native power of the poet, and his fitness
for permanent life, is the strength of resistance in the public
taste. Whatever is too original will be hated at the first.
It must slowly mould a public for itself, and the resistance
of the early thoughtless judgements must be overcome by
a counter resistance to itself, in a better audience slowly
mustering against the first. Forty and seven years [1] it is 30
since William Wordsworth first appeared as an author.
Twenty of those years he was the scoff of the world, and his
poetry a by-word of scorn. Since then, and more than once,

[1] Written in 1845.

senates have rung with acclamations to the echo of his name.
Now at this moment, whilst we are talking about him, he has
entered upon his seventy-sixth year. For himself, according
to the course of nature, he cannot be far from his setting ;
but his poetry is only now clearing the clouds that gathered
about its rising. Meditative poetry is perhaps that province
of literature which will ultimately maintain most power
amongst the generations which are coming ; but in this
department, at least, there is little competition to be appre-
10 hended by Wordsworth from anything that has appeared
since the death of Shakespeare.

Selections from

WORDSWORTH'S

POETRY and PROSE

REMEMBRANCE

OF

COLLINS

COMPOSED UPON THE THAMES NEAR RICHMOND

Composed 1789.—Published 1798

GLIDE gently, thus for ever glide,
O Thames! that other bards may see
As lovely visions by thy side
As now, fair river! come to me.
O glide, fair stream! for ever so,5
Thy quiet soul on all bestowing,
Till all our minds for ever flow
As thy deep waters now are flowing.

Vain thought!—Yet be as now thou art,
That in thy waters may be seen10
The image of a poet's heart,
How bright, how solemn, how serene!
Such as did once the Poet bless,
Who, murmuring here a later ditty,
Could find no refuge from distress15
But in the milder grief of pity.

Now let us, as we float along,
For *him* suspend the dashing oar;
And pray that never child of song
May know that Poet's sorrows more.20
How calm! how still! the only sound,
The dripping of the oar suspended!
—The evening darkness gathers round
By virtue's holiest Powers attended.

L I N E S

WRITTEN IN EARLY SPRING

Composed 1798.—Published 1798

I HEARD a thousand blended notes,
While in a grove I sate reclined,
In that sweet mood when pleasant thoughts
Bring sad thoughts to the mind.

To her fair works did Nature link   5
The human soul that through me ran ;
And much it grieved my heart to think
What man has made ot man.

Through primrose tufts, in that green bower,
The periwinkle trailed its wreaths ;   10
And 'tis my faith that every flower
Enjoys the air it breathes.

The birds around me hopped and played,
Their thoughts I cannot measure :—
But the least motion which they made,   15
It seemed a thrill of pleasure.

The budding twigs spread out their fan,
To catch the breezy air ;
And I must think, do all I can,
That there was pleasure there.   20

If this belief from heaven be sent,
If such be Nature's holy plan,
Have I not reason to lament
What man has made of man ?

T O
M Y   S I S T E R

Composed 1798.—Published 1798

It is the first mild day of March :
Each minute sweeter than before,
The redbreast sings from the tall larch
That stands beside our door.

There is a blessing in the air,   5
Which seems a sense of joy to yield
To the bare trees, and mountains bare,
And grass in the green field.

My sister ! ('tis a wish of mine)
Now that our morning meal is done,   10
Make haste, your morning task resign ;
Come forth and feel the sun.

Edward will come with you ;—and, pray,
Put on with speed your woodland dress ;
And bring no book : for this one day   15
We'll give to idleness.

No joyless forms shall regulate
Our living calendar :
We from to-day, my Friend, will date
The opening of the year.   20

Love, now a universal birth,
From heart to heart is stealing,
From earth to man, from man to earth :
—It is the hour of feeling.

One moment now may give us more   25
Than years of toiling reason :
Our minds shall drink at every pore
The spirit of the season.

Some silent laws our hearts will make,
Which they shall long obey:⠀⠀⠀⠀⠀⠀⠀⠀30
We for the year to come may take
Our temper from to-day.

And from the blessed power that rolls
About, below, above,
We'll frame the measure of our souls:⠀⠀⠀35
They shall be tuned to love.

Then come, my Sister! come, I pray,
With speed put on your woodland dress;
And bring no book: for this one day
We'll give to idleness.⠀⠀⠀⠀⠀⠀⠀⠀⠀⠀40

LINES

COMPOSED A FEW MILES ABOVE

TINTERN ABBEY,

ON REVISITING THE BANKS OF THE WYE DURING

A TOUR.

July 13, 1798

Composed 1798.—Published 1798⠀⠀Time.

FIVE years have past; five summers, with the length
Of five long winters! and again I hear
These waters, rolling from their mountain-springs
With a soft inland murmur.—Once again
Do I behold these steep and lofty cliffs,⠀⠀⠀⠀5
That on a wild secluded scene impress
Thoughts of more deep seclusion; and connect
The landscape with the quiet of the sky.
The day is come when I again repose⠀effect of nature. (Rest)
Here, under this dark sycamore, and view⠀⠀Peacefulness
These plots of cottage-ground, these orchard-tufts,⠀10

Hypnotic absorbtion into poem
through blank verse.

Which at this season, with their unripe fruits,
Are clad in one green hue, and lose themselves
'Mid groves and copses. Once again I see
These hedge-rows, hardly hedge-rows, little lines   15
Of sportive wood run wild : these pastoral farms,
Green to the very door ; and wreaths of smoke
Sent up, in silence, from among the trees !
With some uncertain notice, as might seem
Of vagrant dwellers in the houseless woods,   20
Or of some Hermit's cave, where by his fire
The Hermit sits alone.
                These beauteous forms,
Through a long absence, have not been to me
As is a landscape to a blind man's eye :
But oft, in lonely rooms, and 'mid the din   25
Of towns and cities, I have owed to them,
In hours of weariness, sensations sweet,
Felt in the blood, and felt along the heart ;
And passing even into my purer mind,
With tranquil restoration :—feelings too   30
Of unremembered pleasure : such, perhaps,
As have no slight or trivial influence
On that best portion of a good man's life,
His little, nameless, unremembered, acts
Of kindness and of love. Nor less, I trust,   35
To them I may have owed another gift,
Of aspect more sublime ; that blessed mood,
In which the burthen of the mystery,
In which the heavy and the weary weight
Of all this unintelligible world,   40
Is lightened :—that serene and blessed mood,
In which the affections gently lead us on,—
Until, the breath of this corporeal frame
And even the motion of our human blood
Almost suspended, we are laid asleep   45

In body, and become a living soul :
While with an eye made quiet by the power
Of harmony, and the deep power of joy,
We see into the life of things.
                              If this
Be but a vain belief, yet, oh ! how oft—   50
In darkness and amid the many shapes
Of joyless daylight ; when the fretful stir
Unprofitable, and the fever of the world,
Have hung upon the beatings of my heart—
How oft, in spirit, have I turned to thee,   55
O sylvan Wye ! thou wanderer thro' the woods,
How often has my spirit turned to thee !

And now, with gleams of half-extinguished thought,
With many recognitions dim and faint,
And somewhat of a sad perplexity,   60
The picture of the mind revives again :
While here I stand, not only with the sense
Of present pleasure, but with pleasing thoughts
That in this moment there is life and food
For future years. And so I dare to hope,   65
Though changed, no doubt, from what I was when first
I came among these hills ; when like a roe
I bounded o'er the mountains, by the sides
Of the deep rivers, and the lonely streams,
Wherever nature led : more like a man   70
Flying from something that he dreads than one
Who sought the thing he loved. For nature then
(The coarser pleasures of my boyish days,
And their glad animal movements all gone by)
To me was all in all.—I cannot paint   75
What then I was. The sounding cataract
Haunted me like a passion : the tall rock,
The mountain, and the deep and gloomy wood,

Their colours and their forms, were then to me
An appetite; a feeling and a love,   80
That had no need of a remoter charm,
By thought supplied, nor any interest
Unborrowed from the eye.—That time is past,
And all its aching joys are now no more,
And all its dizzy raptures. Not for this   85
Faint I, nor mourn nor murmur; other gifts
Have followed; for such loss, I would believe,
Abundant recompense. For I have learned
To look on nature, not as in the hour
Of thoughtless youth; but hearing oftentimes   90
The still, sad music of humanity,
Nor harsh nor grating, though of ample power
To chasten and subdue. And I have felt
A presence that disturbs me with the joy
Of elevated thoughts; a sense sublime   95
Of something far more deeply interfused,
Whose dwelling is the light of setting suns,
And the round ocean and the living air,
And the blue sky, and in the mind of man:
A motion and a spirit, that impels   100
All thinking things, all objects of all thought,
And rolls through all things. Therefore am I still
A lover of the meadows and the woods,
And mountains; and of all that we behold
From this green earth; of all the mighty world   105
Of eye, and ear,—both what they half create,
And what perceive; well pleased to recognise
In nature and the language of the sense
The anchor of my purest thoughts, the nurse,
The guide, the guardian of my heart, and soul   110
Of all my moral being.
                              Nor perchance,
If I were not thus taught, should I the more

Suffer my genial spirits to decay:
For thou art with me here upon the banks
Of this fair river; thou my dearest Friend,   115
My dear, dear Friend; and in thy voice I catch
The language of my former heart, and read
My former pleasures in the shooting lights
Of thy wild eyes. Oh! yet a little while
May I behold in thee what I was once,   120
My dear, dear Sister! and this prayer I make,
Knowing that Nature never did betray
The heart that loved her; 'tis her privilege,
Through all the years of this our life, to lead
From joy to joy: for she can so inform   125
The mind that is within us, so impress
With quietness and beauty, and so feed
With lofty thoughts, that neither evil tongues,
Rash judgments, nor the sneers of selfish men,
Nor greetings where no kindness is, nor all   130
The dreary intercourse of daily life,
Shall e'er prevail against us, or disturb
Our cheerful faith, that all which we behold
Is full of blessings. Therefore let the moon
Shine on thee in thy solitary walk;   135
And let the misty mountain-winds be free
To blow against thee: and, in after years,
When these wild ecstasies shall be matured
Into a sober pleasure; when thy mind
Shall be a mansion for all lovely forms,   140
Thy memory be as a dwelling-place
For all sweet sounds and harmonies; oh! then,
If solitude, or fear, or pain, or grief,
Should be thy portion, with what healing thoughts
Of tender joy wilt thou remember me,   145
And these my exhortations! Nor, perchance—
If I should be where I no more can hear

Thy voice, nor catch from thy wild eyes these gleams
Of past existence—wilt thou then forget
That on the banks of this delightful stream   150
We stood together ; and that I, so long
A worshipper of Nature, hither came
Unwearied in that service : rather say
With warmer love—oh ! with far deeper zeal
Of holier love. Nor wilt thou then forget   155
That after many wanderings, many years
Of absence, these steep woods and lofty cliffs,
And this green pastoral landscape, were to me
More dear, both for themselves and for thy sake !

T H E

OLD CUMBERLAND BEGGAR

Composed 1797.—Published 1800

I SAW an aged Beggar in my walk ;
And he was seated, by the highway side,
On a low structure of rude masonry
Built at the foot of a huge hill, that they
Who lead their horses down the steep rough road   5
May thence remount at ease. The aged Man
Had placed his staff across the broad smooth stone
That overlays the pile ; and, from a bag
All white with flour, the dole of village dames,
He drew his scraps and fragments, one by one ;   10
And scanned them with a fixed and serious look
Of idle computation. In the sun,
Upon the second step of that small pile,
Surrounded by those wild unpeopled hills,
He sat, and ate his food in solitude :   15
And ever, scattered from his palsied hand,
That, still attempting to prevent the waste,

Was baffled still, the crumbs in little showers
Fell on the ground ; and the small mountain birds,
Not venturing yet to peck their destined meal,   20
Approached within the length of half his staff.

Him from my childhood have I known ; and then
He was so old, he seems not older now ;
He travels on, a solitary Man,
So helpless in appearance, that for him   25
The sauntering Horseman throws not with a slack
And careless hand his alms upon the ground,
But stops,—that he may safely lodge the coin
Within the old Man's hat ; nor quits him so,
But still, when he has given his horse the rein,   30
Watches the aged Beggar with a look
Sidelong, and half-reverted. She who tends
The toll-gate, when in summer at her door
She turns her wheel, if on the road she sees
The aged Beggar coming, quits her work,   35
And lifts the latch for him that he may pass.
The post-boy, when his rattling wheels o'ertake
The aged Beggar in the woody lane,
Shouts to him from behind ; and, if thus warned
The old man does not change his course, the boy   40
Turns with less noisy wheels to the roadside,
And passes gently by, without a curse
Upon his lips or anger at his heart.

He travels on, a solitary Man ;
His age has no companion. On the ground   45
His eyes are turned, and, as he moves along,
They move along the ground ; and, evermore,
Instead of common and habitual sight
Of fields with rural works, of hill and dale,
And the blue sky, one little span of earth   50
Is all his prospect. Thus, from day to day.

Bow-bent, his eyes for ever on the ground,
He plies his weary journey; seeing still,
And seldom knowing that he sees, some straw,
Some scattered leaf, or marks which, in one track, 55
The nails of cart or chariot-wheel have left
Impressed on the white road,—in the same line,
At distance still the same.   Poor Traveller !
His staff trails with him ; scarcely do his feet
Disturb the summer dust ; he is so still 60
In look and motion, that the cottage curs,
Ere he has passed the door, will turn away,
Weary of barking at him.   Boys and girls,
The vacant and the busy, maids and youths,
And urchins newly breeched—all pass him by : 65
Him even the slow-paced waggon leaves behind.

But deem not this Man useless.—Statesmen ! ye
Who are so restless in your wisdom, ye
Who have a broom still ready in your hands
To rid the world of nuisances ; ye proud, 70
Heart-swoln, while in your pride ye contemplate
Your talents, power, or wisdom, deem him not
A burthen of the earth ! 'Tis Nature's law
That none, the meanest of created things,
Of forms created the most vile and brute, 75
The dullest or most noxious, should exist
Divorced from good—a spirit and pulse of good,
A life and soul, to every mode of being
Inseparably linked.   Then be assured
That least of all can aught—that ever owned 80
The heaven-regarding eye and front sublime
Which man is born to—sink, howe'er depressed,
So low as to be scorned without a sin ;
Without offence to God cast out of view ;
Like the dry remnant of a garden-flower 85

Whose seeds are shed, or as an implement
Worn out and worthless. While from door to door,
This old Man creeps, the villagers in him
Behold a record which together binds
Past deeds and offices of charity,   90
Else unremembered, and so keeps alive
The kindly mood in hearts which lapse of years,
And that half-wisdom half-experience gives,
Make slow to feel, and by sure steps resign
To selfishness and cold oblivious cares.   95
Among the farms and solitary huts,
Hamlets and thinly-scattered villages,
Where'er the aged Beggar takes his rounds,
The mild necessity of use compels
To acts of love ; and habit does the work   100
Of reason ; yet prepares that after-joy
Which reason cherishes. And thus the soul,
By that sweet taste of pleasure unpursued,
Doth find herself insensibly disposed
To virtue and true goodness.
                              Some there are,   105
By their good works exalted, lofty minds,
And meditative, authors of delight
And happiness, which to the end of time
Will live, and spread, and kindle : even such minds
In childhood, from this solitary Being,   110
Or from like wanderer, haply have received
(A thing more precious far than all that books
Or the solicitudes of love can do !)
That first mild touch of sympathy and thought,
In which they found their kindred with a world   115
Where want and sorrow were. The easy man
Who sits at his own door,—and, like the pear
That overhangs his head from the green wall,
Feeds in the sunshine ; the robust and young,

The prosperous and unthinking, they who live   120
Sheltered, and flourish in a little grove
Of their own kindred ;—all behold in him
A silent monitor, which on their minds
Must needs impress a transitory thought
Of self-congratulation, to the heart   125
Of each recalling his peculiar boons,
His charters and exemptions ; and, perchance,
Though he to no one give the fortitude
And circumspection needful to preserve
His present blessings, and to husband up   130
The respite of the season, he, at least,
And 'tis no vulgar service, makes them felt.

  Yet further.——Many, I believe, there are
Who live a life of virtuous decency,
Men who can hear the Decalogue and feel   135
No self-reproach ; who of the moral law
Established in the land where they abide
Are strict observers ; and not negligent
In acts of love to those with whom they dwell,
Their kindred, and the children of their blood.   140
Praise be to such, and to their slumbers peace !
—But of the poor man ask, the abject poor ;
Go, and demand of him, if there be here
In this cold abstinence from evil deeds,
And these inevitable charities,   145
Wherewith to satisfy the human soul ?
No—man is dear to man ; the poorest poor
Long for some moments in a weary life
When they can know and feel that they have been,
Themselves, the fathers and the dealers-out   150
Of some small blessings ; have been kind to such
As needed kindness, for this single cause,
That we have all of us one human heart.

—Such pleasure is to one kind Being known,
My neighbour, when with punctual care, each week,
Duly as Friday comes, though pressed herself   156
By her own wants, she from her store of meal
Takes one unsparing handful for the scrip
Of this old Mendicant, and, from her door
Returning with exhilarated heart,   160
Sits by her fire, and builds her hope in heaven.

Then let him pass, a blessing on his head !
And while in that vast solitude to which
The tide of things has borne him, he appears
To breathe and live but for himself alone,   165
Unblamed, uninjured, let him bear about
The good which the benignant law of Heaven
Has hung around him : and, while life is his,
Still let him prompt the unlettered villagers
To tender offices and pensive thoughts.   170
—Then let him pass, a blessing on his head !
And, long as he can wander, let him breathe
The freshness of the valleys ; let his blood
Struggle with frosty air and winter snows ;
And let the chartered wind that sweeps the heath   175
Beat his grey locks against his withered face.
Reverence the hope whose vital anxiousness
Gives the last human interest to his heart.
May never HOUSE, misnamed of INDUSTRY,
Make him a captive !—for that pent-up din,   180
Those life-consuming sounds that clog the air,
Be his the natural silence of old age !
Let him be free of mountain solitudes ;
And have around him, whether heard or not,
The pleasant melody of woodland birds.   185
Few are his pleasures : if his eyes have now
Been doomed so long to settle upon earth

That not without some effort they behold
The countenance of the horizontal sun,
Rising or setting, let the light at least   190
Find a free entrance to their languid orbs,
And let him, *where* and *when* he will, sit down
Beneath the trees, or on a grassy bank
Of highway side, and with the little birds
Share his chance-gathered meal ; and, finally,   195
As in the eye of Nature he has lived,
So in the eye of Nature let him die !

EXPOSTULATION

AND

REPLY

Composed 1798.—Published 1798

' WHY, William, on that old grey stone,
Thus for the length of half a day,
Why, William, sit you thus alone,
And dream your time away ?

' Where are your books ?—that light bequeathed   5
To Beings else forlorn and blind !
Up ! up ! and drink the spirit breathed
From dead men to their kind.

' You look round on your Mother Earth,
As if she for no purpose bore you ;   10
As if you were her first-born birth,
And none had lived before you ! '

One morning thus, by Esthwaite lake,
When life was sweet, I knew not why,
To me my good friend Matthew spake,   15
And thus I made reply :

' The eye—it cannot choose but see :
We cannot bid the ear be still ;
Our bodies feel, where'er they be,
Against or with our will.   20

' Nor less I deem that there are Powers
Which of themselves our minds impress ;
That we can feed this mind of ours
In a wise passiveness.

' Think you, 'mid all this mighty sum   25
Of things for ever speaking,
That nothing of itself will come,
But we must still be seeking ?

' —Then ask not wherefore, here, alone,
Conversing as I may,   30
I sit upon this old grey stone,
And dream my time away.'

THE TABLES TURNED

AN EVENING SCÈNE ON THÈ SAME SUBJÉCT

Composed 1798.—Published 1798

Up ! up ! my Friend, and quit your books ;
Or surely you'll grow double :
Up ! up ! my Friend, and clear your looks ;
Why all this toil and trouble ?

The sun, above the mountain's head,   5
A freshening lustre mellow
Through all the long green fields has spread,
His first sweet evening yellow.

Books ! 'tis a dull and endless strife :
Come, hear the woodland linnet,   10
How sweet his music ! on my life,
There 's more of wisdom in it.

And hark ! how blithe the throstle sings !
He, too, is no mean preacher :
Come forth into the light of things,   15
Let Nature be your Teacher.

She has a world of ready wealth,
Our minds and hearts to bless—
Spontaneous wisdom breathed by health,
Truth breathed by cheerfulness.   20

One impulse from a vernal wood
May teach you more of man,
Of moral evil and of good,
Than all the sages can.

Sweet is the lore which Nature brings ;   25
Our meddling intellect
Mis-shapes the beauteous forms of things :—
We murder to dissect.

Enough of Science and of Art ;
Close up those barren leaves ;   30
Come forth, and bring with you a heart
That watches and receives.

THE FOUNTAIN

A CONVERSATION

Composed 1799.—Published 1800

WE talked with open heart, and tongue
Affectionate and true,
A pair of friends, though I was young,
And Matthew seventy-two.

We lay beneath a spreading oak,   5
Beside a mossy seat ;
And from the turf a fountain broke,
And gurgled at our feet.

'Now, Matthew!' said I, 'let us match
This water's pleasant tune   10
With some old border-song, or catch
That suits a summer's noon;

'Or of the church-clock and the chimes
Sing here beneath the shade,
That half-mad thing of witty rhymes   15
Which you last April made!'

In silence Matthew lay, and eyed
The spring beneath the tree;
And thus the dear old Man replied,
The grey-haired man of glee: 20

'No check, no stay, this Streamlet fears;
How merrily it goes!
'Twill murmur on a thousand years,
And flow as now it flows.

'And here, on this delightful day,   25
I cannot choose but think
How oft, a vigorous man, I lay
Beside this fountain's brink.

'My eyes are dim with childish tears,
My heart is idly stirred,   30
For the same sound is in my ears
Which in those days I heard.

'Thus fares it still in our decay:
And yet the wiser mind
Mourns less for what age takes away   35
Than what it leaves behind.

'The blackbird amid leafy trees,
The lark above the hill,
Let loose their carols when they please,
Are quiet when they will.   40

' With Nature never do *they* wage
A foolish strife ; they see
A happy youth, and their old age
Is beautiful and free :

' But we are pressed by heavy laws ;   45
And often, glad no more,
We wear a face of joy, because
We have been glad of yore.

' If there be one who need bemoan
His kindred laid in earth,   50
The household hearts that were his own ;
It is the man of mirth.

' My days, my Friend, are almost gone,
My life has been approved,
And many love me ! but by none   55
Am I enough beloved.'

' Now both himself and me he wrongs,
The man who thus complains !
I live and sing my idle songs
Upon these happy plains ;   60

' And, Matthew, for thy children dead
I 'll be a son to thee ! '
At this he grasped my hand, and said,
' Alas ! that cannot be.'

We rose up from the fountain side ;   65
And down the smooth descent
Of the green sheep-track did we glide ;
And through the wood we went ;

And, ere we came to Leonard's rock,
He sang those witty rhymes   70
About the crazy old church-clock,
And the bewildered chimes.

INFLUENCE OF NATURAL OBJECTS

IN CALLING FORTH AND STRENGTHENING THE IMAGINATION IN
BOYHOOD AND EARLY YOUTH

Composed 1799.—Published in *The Friend*, Dec. 28, 1809 ; ed. 1815

WISDOM and Spirit of the universe !
Thou Soul, that art the Eternity of thought !
And giv'st to forms and images a breath
And everlasting motion ! not in vain,
By day or star-light, thus from my first dawn   5
Of childhood didst thou intertwine for me
The passions that build up our human soul ;
Not with the mean and vulgar works of Man ;
But with high objects, with enduring things,
With life and nature ; purifying thus   10
The elements of feeling and of thought,
And sanctifying by such discipline
Both pain and fear,—until we recognise
A grandeur in the beatings of the heart.

Nor was this fellowship vouchsafed to me   15
With stinted kindness. In November days,
When vapours rolling down the valleys made
A lonely scene more lonesome ; among woods
At noon ; and 'mid the calm of summer nights,
When, by the margin of the trembling lake,   20
Beneath the gloomy hills, homeward I went
In solitude, such intercourse was mine :
Mine was it in the fields both day and night,
And by the waters, all the summer long.
And in the frosty season, when the sun   25
Was set, and, visible for many a mile,
The cottage-windows through the twilight blazed.
I heeded not the summons : happy time

It was indeed for all of us ; for me
It was a time of rapture ! Clear and loud   30
The village-clock tolled six—I wheeled about,
Proud and exulting like an untired horse
That cares not for his home.—All shod with steel
We hissed along the polished ice, in games
Confederate, imitative of the chase   35
And woodland pleasures,—the resounding horn,
The pack loud-chiming, and the hunted hare.
So through the darkness and the cold we flew,
And not a voice was idle : with the din
Smitten, the precipices rang aloud ;   40
The leafless trees and every icy crag
Tinkled like iron ; while far-distant hills
Into the tumult sent an alien sound
Of melancholy not unnoticed, while the stars,
Eastward, were sparkling clear, and in the west   45
The orange sky of evening died away.

Not seldom from the uproar I retired
Into a silent bay, or sportively
Glanced sideway, leaving the tumultuous throng,
To cut across the reflex of a star ;   50
Image that, flying still before me, gleamed
Upon the glassy plain : and oftentimes,
When we had given our bodies to the wind,
And all the shadowy banks on either side
Came sweeping through the darkness, spinning still 55
The rapid line of motion, then at once
Have I, reclining back upon my heels,
Stopped short ; yet still the solitary cliffs
Wheeled by me—even as if the earth had rolled
With visible motion her diurnal round !   60
Behind me did they stretch in solemn train,
Feebler and feebler, and I stood and watched
Till all was tranquil as a summer sea.

NUTTING

Composed 1799.—Published 1800

—————————————It seems a day
(I speak of one from many singled out)
One of those heavenly days that cannot die;
When, in the eagerness of boyish hope,
I left our cottage-threshold, sallying forth   5
With a huge wallet o'er my shoulders slung,
A nutting-crook in hand; and turned my steps
Tow'rd some far-distant wood, a Figure quaint,
Tricked out in proud disguise of cast-off weeds
Which for that service had been husbanded,   10
By exhortation of my frugal Dame—
Motley accoutrement, of power to smile
At thorns, and brakes, and brambles,—and in truth
More ragged than need was! O'er pathless rocks,
Through beds of matted fern, and tangled thickets, 15
Forcing my way, I came to one dear nook
Unvisited, where not a broken bough
Drooped with its withered leaves, ungracious sign
Of devastation; but the hazels rose
Tall and erect, with tempting clusters hung,   20
A virgin scene!—A little while I stood,
Breathing with such suppression of the heart
As joy delights in; and with wise restraint
Voluptuous, fearless of a rival, eyed
The banquet;—or beneath the trees I sate   25
Among the flowers, and with the flowers I played;
A temper known to those who, after long
And weary expectation, have been blest
With sudden happiness beyond all hope.
Perhaps it was a bower beneath whose leaves   30
The violets of five seasons re-appear
And fade, unseen by any human eye;

Where fairy water-breaks do murmur on
For ever; and I saw the sparkling foam,
And—with my cheek on one of those green stones   35
That, fleeced with moss, under the shady trees,
Lay round me, scattered like a flock of sheep—
I heard the murmur and the murmuring sound,
In that sweet mood when pleasure loves to pay
Tribute to ease; and, of its joy secure,   40
The heart luxuriates with indifferent things,
Wasting its kindliness on stocks and stones,
And on the vacant air. Then up I rose,
And dragged to earth both branch and bough, with crash
And merciless ravage: and the shady nook   45
Of hazels, and the green and mossy bower,
Deformed and sullied, patiently gave up
Their quiet being: and unless I now
Confound my present feelings with the past,
Ere from the mutilated bower I turned   50
Exulting, rich beyond the wealth of kings,
I felt a sense of pain when I beheld
The silent trees, and saw the intruding sky.—
Then, dearest Maiden, move along these shades
In gentleness of heart; with gentle hand   55
Touch—for there is a spirit in the woods.

THE SIMPLON PASS

Composed 1799 (? 1804).—Published 1845

————Brook and road
Were fellow-travellers in this gloomy Pass,
And with them did we journey several hours
At a slow step. The immeasurable height
Of woods decaying, never to be decayed,   5
The stationary blasts of waterfalls,
And in the narrow rent, at every turn,

Winds thwarting winds bewildered and forlorn,
The torrents shooting from the clear blue sky,
The rocks that muttered close upon our ears,   10
Black drizzling crags that spake by the wayside
As if a voice were in them, the sick sight
And giddy prospect of the raving stream,
The unfettered clouds and regions of the heavens,
Tumult and peace, the darkness and the light—   15
Were all like workings of one mind, the features
Of the same face, blossoms upon one tree,
Characters of the great Apocalypse,
The types and symbols of Eternity,
Of first, and last, and midst, and without end.   20

[L U C Y]

Composed 1799.—Published 1800

STRANGE fits of passion have I known :
And I will dare to tell,
But in the Lover's ear alone,
What once to me befell.

When she I loved looked every day   5
Fresh as a rose in June,
I to her cottage bent my way,
Beneath an evening-moon.

Upon the moon I fixed my eye,
All over the wide lea ;   10
With quickening pace my horse drew nigh
Those paths so dear to me.

And now we reached the orchard-plot :
And, as we climbed the hill,
The sinking moon to Lucy's cot   15
Came near, and nearer still.

In one of those sweet dreams I slept,
Kind Nature's gentlest boon!
And all the while my eyes I kept
On the descending moon.   20

My horse moved on ; hoof after hoof
He raised, and never stopped :
When down behind the cottage roof,
At once, the bright moon dropped.

What fond and wayward thoughts will slide 25
Into a Lover's head !
' O mercy ! ' to myself I cried,
' If Lucy should be dead ! '

Composed 1799.—Published 1800

SHE dwelt among the untrodden ways
    Beside the springs of Dove,
A Maid whom there were none to praise
    And very few to love :

A violet by a mossy stone   5
    Half hidden from the eye !
—Fair as a star, when only one
    Is shining in the sky.

She lived unknown, and few could know
    When Lucy ceased to be ;   10
But she is in her grave, and, oh,
    The difference to me !

Composed 1799.—Published 1807

I TRAVELLED among unknown men,
    In lands beyond the sea ;
Nor, England ! did I know till then
    What love I bore to thee.

'Tis past, that melancholy dream !   5
  Nor will I quit thy shore
A second time ; for still I seem
  To love thee more and more.

Among thy mountains did I feel
  The joy of my desire ;   10
And she I cherished turned her wheel
  Beside an English fire.

Thy mornings showed, thy nights concealed,
  The bowers where Lucy played ;
And thine too is the last green field   15
  That Lucy's eyes surveyed.

Composed 1799.—Published 1800

THREE years she grew in sun and shower,
Then Nature said, ' A lovelier flower
On earth was never sown ;
This Child I to myself will take ;
She shall be mine, and I will make   5
A Lady of my own.

' Myself will to my darling be
Both law and impulse : and with me
The Girl, in rock and plain,
In earth and heaven, in glade and bower,   10
Shall feel an overseeing power
To kindle or restrain.

' She shall be sportive as the fawn
That wild with glee across the lawn
Or up the mountain springs ;   15
And hers shall be the breathing balm,
And hers the silence and the calm
Of mute insensate things.

'The floating clouds their state shall lend
To her; for her the willow bend;   20
Nor shall she fail to see
Even in the motions of the Storm
Grace that shall mould the Maiden's form
By silent sympathy.

'The stars of midnight shall be dear   25
To her; and she shall lean her ear
In many a secret place
Where rivulets dance their wayward round,
And beauty born of murmuring sound
Shall pass into her face.   30

'And vital feelings of delight
Shall rear her form to stately height,
Her virgin bosom swell;
Such thoughts to Lucy I will give
While she and I together live   35
Here in this happy dell.'

Thus Nature spake—The work was done—
How soon my Lucy's race was run!
She died, and left to me
This heath, this calm, and quiet scene;   40
The memory of what has been,
And never more will be.

Composed 1799.—Published 1800

A SLUMBER did my spirit seal;
  I had no human fears:
She seemed a thing that could not feel
  The touch of earthly years.

No motion has she now, no force;   5
  She neither hears nor sees;   *daily*
Rolled round in earth's diurnal course.
  With rocks, and stones, and trees.

She is absorbed into nature itself

MICHAEL

A PASTORAL POEM

Composed October 11–December 9, 1800.—Published 1800

IF from the public way you turn your steps
Up the tumultuous brook of Green-head Ghyll,
You will suppose that with an upright path
Your feet must struggle ; in such bold ascent
The pastoral mountains front you, face to face.   5
But, courage ! for around that boisterous brook
The mountains have all opened out themselves,
And made a hidden valley of their own.
No habitation can be seen : but they
Who journey thither find themselves alone   10
With a few sheep, with rocks and stones, and kites
That overhead are sailing in the sky.
It is in truth an utter solitude ;
Nor should I have made mention of this Dell
But for one object which you might pass by,   15
Might see and notice not. Beside the brook
Appears a straggling heap of unhewn stones !
And to that simple object appertains
A story—unenriched with strange events,
Yet not unfit, I deem, for the fireside,   20
Or for the summer shade. It was the first
Of those domestic tales that spake to me
Of Shepherds, dwellers in the valleys, men
Whom I already loved ;—not verily
For their own sakes, but for the fields and hills   25
Where was their occupation and abode.
And hence this Tale, while I was yet a Boy
Careless of books, yet having felt the power
Of Nature, by the gentle agency
Of natural objects, led me on to feel   30

For passions that were not my own, and think
(At random and imperfectly indeed)
On man, the heart of man, and human life.
Therefore, although it be a history
Homely and rude, I will relate the same   35
For the delight of a few natural hearts ;
And, with yet fonder feeling, for the sake
Of youthful Poets, who among these hills
Will be my second self when I am gone.

UPON the forest-side in Grasmere Vale   40
There dwelt a Shepherd, Michael was his name ;
An old man, stout of heart, and strong of limb.
His bodily frame had been from youth to age
Of an unusual strength : his mind was keen,
Intense, and frugal, apt for all affairs,   45
And in his shepherd's calling he was prompt
And watchful more than ordinary men.
Hence had he learned the meaning of all winds,
Of blasts of every tone ; and oftentimes,
When others heeded not, He heard the South   50
Make subterraneous music, like the noise
Of bagpipers on distant Highland hills.
The Shepherd, at such warning, of his flock
Bethought him, and he to himself would say,
' The winds are now devising work for me ! '   55
And, truly, at all times, the storm, that drives
The traveller to a shelter, summoned him
Up to the mountains : he had been alone
Amid the heart of many thousand mists,
That came to him, and left him, on the heights.   60
So lived he till his eightieth year was past.
And grossly that man errs, who should suppose
That the green valleys, and the streams and rocks,
Were things indifferent to the Shepherd's thoughts.

Fields, where with cheerful spirits he had breathed   65
The common air ; hills, which with vigorous step
He had so often climbed ; which had impressed
So many incidents upon his mind
Of hardship, skill or courage, joy or fear ;
Which, like a book, preserved the memory   70
Of the dumb animals, whom he had saved,
Had fed or sheltered, linking to such acts
The certainty of honourable gain ;
Those fields, those hills—what could they less ? had laid
Strong hold on his affections, were to him   75
A pleasurable feeling of blind love,
The pleasure which there is in life itself.

His days had not been passed in singleness.
His Helpmate was a comely matron, old—
Though younger than himself full twenty years.   80
She was a woman of a stirring life,
Whose heart was in her house : two wheels she had
Of antique form ; this large, for spinning wool ;
That small, for flax ; and, if one wheel had rest,
It was because the other was at work.   85
The Pair had but one inmate in their house,
An only Child, who had been born to them
When Michael, telling o'er his years, began
To deem that he was old,—in shepherd's phrase,
With one foot in the grave. This only Son,   90
With two brave sheep-dogs tried in many a storm,
The one of an inestimable worth,
Made all their household. I may truly say,
That they were as a proverb in the vale
For endless industry. When day was gone,   95
And from their occupations out of doors
The Son and Father were come home, even then,
Their labour did not cease ; unless when all

Turned to the cleanly supper-board, and there,
Each with a mess of pottage and skimmed milk,   100
Sat round the basket piled with oaten cakes,
And their plain home-made cheese. Yet when the meal
Was ended, Luke (for so the Son was named)
And his old Father both betook themselves
To such convenient work as might employ   105
Their hands by the fire-side ; perhaps to card
Wool for the Housewife's spindle, or repair
Some injury done to sickle, flail, or scythe,
Or other implement of house or field.

Down from the ceiling, by the chimney's edge,   110
That in our ancient uncouth country style
With huge and black projection overbrowed
Large space beneath, as duly as the light
Of day grew dim the Housewife hung a lamp ;
An aged utensil, which had performed   115
Service beyond all others of its kind.
Early at evening did it burn—and late,
Surviving comrade of uncounted hours,
Which, going by from year to year, had found,
And left, the couple neither gay perhaps   120
Nor cheerful, yet with objects and with hopes,
Living a life of eager industry.
And now, when Luke had reached his eighteenth year,
There by the light of this old lamp they sate,
Father and Son, while far into the night   125
The Housewife plied her own peculiar work,
Making the cottage through the silent hours
Murmur as with the sound of summer flies.
This light was famous in its neighbourhood,
And was a public symbol of the life   130
That thrifty Pair had lived. For, as it chanced
Their cottage on a plot of rising ground

Stood single, with large prospect, north and south,
High into Easedale, up to Dunmail-Raise,
And westward to the village near the lake ;   135
And from this constant light, so regular,
And so far seen, the House itself, by all
Who dwelt within the limits of the vale,
Both old and young, was named THE EVENING STAR.

Thus living on through such a length of years,   140
The Shepherd, if he loved himself, must needs
Have loved his Helpmate ; but to Michael's heart
This son of his old age was yet more dear—
Less from instinctive tenderness, the same
Fond spirit that blindly works in the blood of all— 145
Than that a child, more than all other gifts
That earth can offer to declining man,
Brings hope with it, and forward-looking thoughts,
And stirrings of inquietude, when they
By tendency of nature needs must fail.   150
Exceeding was the love he bare to him,
His heart and his heart's joy ! For oftentimes
Old Michael, while he was a babe in arms,
Had done him female service, not alone
For pastime and delight, as is the use   155
Of fathers, but with patient mind enforced
To acts of tenderness ; and he had rocked
His cradle, as with a woman's gentle hand.

And in a later time, ere yet the Boy
Had put on boy's attire, did Michael love,   160
Albeit of a stern unbending mind,
To have the Young-one in his sight, when he
Wrought in the field, or on his shepherd's stool
Sate with a fettered sheep before him stretched
Under the large old oak, that near his door   165

Stood single, and, from matchless depth of shade,
Chosen for the Shearer's covert from the sun,
Thence in our rustic dialect was called
The CLIPPING TREE,[1] a name which yet it bears.
There, while they two were sitting in the shade,   170
With others round them, earnest all and blithe,
Would Michael exercise his heart with looks
Of fond correction and reproof bestowed
Upon the Child, if he disturbed the sheep
By catching at their legs, or with his shouts   175
Scared them, while they lay still beneath the shears.

And when by Heaven's good grace the boy grew up
A healthy Lad, and carried in his cheek
Two steady roses that were five years old :
Then Michael from a winter coppice cut   180
With his own hand a sapling, which he hooped
With iron, making it throughout in all
Due requisites a perfect shepherd's staff,
And gave it to the Boy ; wherewith equipt
He as a watchman oftentimes was placed   185
At gate or gap, to stem or turn the flock ;
And, to his office prematurely called,
There stood the urchin, as you will divine,
Something between a hindrance and a help ;
And for this cause not always, I believe,   190
Receiving from his Father hire of praise ;
Though nought was left undone which staff, or voice,
Or looks, or threatening gestures, could perform.

But soon as Luke, full ten years old, could stand
Against the mountain blasts ; and to the heights,   195
Not fearing toil, nor length of weary ways,
He with his Father daily went, and they

[1] Clipping is the word used in the North of England for shearing.

Were as companions, why should I relate
That objects which the Shepherd loved before
Were dearer now? that from the Boy there came   200
Feelings and emanations—things which were
Light to the sun and music to the wind;
And that the old Man's heart seemed born again?

Thus in his Father's sight the Boy grew up:
And now, when he had reached his eighteenth year, 205
He was his comfort and his daily hope.

While in this sort the simple household lived
From day to day, to Michael's ear there came
Distressful tidings.   Long before the time
Of which I speak, the Shepherd had been bound   210
In surety for his brother's son, a man
Of an industrious life, and ample means;
But unforeseen misfortunes suddenly
Had prest upon him; and old Michael now
Was summoned to discharge the forfeiture,   215
A grievous penalty, but little less
Than half his substance.   This unlooked-for claim,
At the first hearing, for a moment took
More hope out of his life than he supposed
That any old man ever could have lost.   220
As soon as he had armed himself with strength
To look his trouble in the face, it seemed
The Shepherd's sole resource to sell at once
A portion of his patrimonial fields.
Such was his first resolve; he thought again,   225
And his heart failed him.   ' Isabel,' said he,
Two evenings after he had heard the news,
' I have been toiling more than seventy years,
And in the open sunshine of God's love
Have we all lived; yet, if these fields of ours   230

Should pass into a stranger's hand, I think
That I could not lie quiet in my grave.
Our lot is a hard lot; the sun himself
Has scarcely been more diligent than I;
And I have lived to be a fool at last   235
To my own family. An evil man
That was, and made an evil choice, if he
Were false to us; and, if he were not false,
There are ten thousand to whom loss like this
Had been no sorrow. I forgive him;—but   240
'Twere better to be dumb than to talk thus.

When I began, my purpose was to speak
Of remedies and of a cheerful hope.
Our Luke shall leave us, Isabel; the land
Shall not go from us, and it shall be free;   245
He shall possess it, free as is the wind
That passes over it. We have, thou know'st,
Another kinsman—he will be our friend
In this distress. He is a prosperous man,
Thriving in trade—and Luke to him shall go,   250
And with his kinsman's help and his own thrift
He quickly will repair this loss, and then
He may return to us. If here he stay,
What can be done? Where every one is poor,
What can be gained?'
                    At this the old Man paused,   255
And Isabel sat silent, for her mind
Was busy, looking back into past times.
There's Richard Bateman, thought she to herself,
He was a parish-boy—at the church-door
They made a gathering for him, shillings, pence,   260
And halfpennies, wherewith the neighbours bought
A basket, which they filled with pedlar's wares;
And, with this basket on his arm, the lad

Went up to London, found a master there,
Who, out of many, chose the trusty boy   265
To go and overlook his merchandise
Beyond the seas ; where he grew wondrous rich,
And left estates and monies to the poor,
And, at his birth-place, built a chapel floored
With marble, which he sent from foreign lands.   270
These thoughts, and many others of like sort,
Passed quickly through the mind of Isabel,
And her face brightened. The old Man was glad,
And thus resumed :—' Well, Isabel ! this scheme
These two days has been meat and drink to me.   275
Far more than we have lost is left us yet.

　We have enough—I wish indeed that I
Were younger ;—but this hope is a good hope.
Make ready Luke's best garments, of the best
Buy for him more, and let us send him forth   280
To-morrow, or the next day, or to-night :
　If he *could* go, the Boy should go to-night.'

　Here Michael ceased, and to the fields went forth
With a light heart. The Housewife for five days
Was restless morn and night, and all day long   285
Wrought on with her best fingers to prepare
Things needful for the journey of her son.
But Isabel was glad when Sunday came
To stop her in her work : for, when she lay
By Michael's side, she through the last two nights 290
Heard him, how he was troubled in his sleep :
And when they rose at morning she could see
That all his hopes were gone. That day at noon
She said to Luke, while they two by themselves
Were sitting at the door, ' Thou must not go :   295
We have no other Child but thee to lose,
None to remember—do not go away,

For if thou leave thy Father he will die.'
The Youth made answer with a jocund voice ;
And Isabel, when she had told her fears,   300
Recovered heart. That evening her best fare
Did she bring forth, and all together sat
Like happy people round a Christmas fire.

With daylight Isabel resumed her work ;
And all the ensuing week the house appeared   305
As cheerful as a grove in Spring : at length
The expected letter from their kinsman came,
With kind assurances that he would do
His utmost for the welfare of the Boy ;
To which, requests were added, that forthwith   310
He might be sent to him. Ten times or more
The letter was read over ; Isabel
Went forth to show it to the neighbours round ;
Nor was there at that time on English land
A prouder heart than Luke's. When Isabel   315
Had to her house returned, the old Man said,
' He shall depart to-morrow.' To this word
The Housewife answered, talking much of things
Which, if at such short notice he should go,
Would surely be forgotten. But at length   320
She gave consent, and Michael was at ease.

Near the tumultuous brook of Green-head Ghyll,
In that deep valley, Michael had designed
To build a Sheep-fold ; and, before he heard
The tidings of his melancholy loss,   325
For this same purpose he had gathered up
A heap of stones, which by the streamlet's edge
Lay thrown together, ready for the work.
With Luke that evening thitherward he walked :
And soon as they had reached the place he stopped, 330

And thus the old Man spake to him :—' My son,
To-morrow thou wilt leave me : with full heart
I look upon thee, for thou art the same
That wert a promise to me ere thy birth,
And all thy life hast been my daily joy.   335
I will relate to thee some little part
Of our two histories ; 'twill do thee good
When thou art from me, even if I should touch
On things thou canst not know of.——After thou
First cam'st into the world—as oft befalls   340
To new-born infants—thou didst sleep away
Two days, and blessings from thy Father's tongue
Then fell upon thee. Day by day passed on,
And still I loved thee with increasing love.
Never to living ear came sweeter sounds   345
Than when I heard thee by our own fireside
First uttering, without words, a natural tune :
While thou, a feeding babe, didst in thy joy
Sing at thy Mother's breast. Month followed month,
And in the open fields my life was passed   350
And on the mountains ; else I think that thou
Hadst been brought up upon thy Father's knees.
But we were playmates, Luke : among these hills,
As well thou knowest, in us the old and young
Have played together, nor with me didst thou   355
Lack any pleasure which a boy can know.'
Luke had a manly heart ; but at these words
He sobbed aloud. The old Man grasped his hand,
And said, ' Nay, do not take it so—I see
That these are things of which I need not speak.   360
—Even to the utmost I have been to thee
A kind and a good Father : and herein
I but repay a gift which I myself
Received at others' hands ; for, though now old
Beyond the common life of man, I still   365

Remember them who loved me in my youth.
Both of them sleep together : here they lived,
As all their Forefathers had done ; and, when
At length their time was come, they were not loth
To give their bodies to the family mould.   370
I wished that thou shouldst live the life they lived,
But 'tis a long time to look back, my Son,
And see so little gain from threescore years.
These fields were burthened when they came to me ;
Till I was forty years of age, not more   375
Than half of my inheritance was mine.
I toiled and toiled ; God blessed me in my work,
And till these three weeks past the land was free.
—It looks as if it never could endure
Another Master. Heaven forgive me, Luke,   380
If I judge ill for thee, but it seems good
That thou shouldst go.'
                    At this the old Man paused ;
Then, pointing to the stones near which they stood,
Thus, after a short silence, he resumed :
' This was a work for us ; and now, my Son,   385
It is a work for me. But, lay one stone—
Here, lay it for me, Luke, with thine own hands.
Nay, Boy, be of good hope ;—we both may live
To see a better day. At eighty-four
I still am strong and hale ;—do thou thy part ;   390
I will do mine.—I will begin again
With many tasks that were resigned to thee :
Up to the heights, and in among the storms,
Will I without thee go again, and do
All works which I was wont to do alone,   395
Before I knew thy face.—Heaven bless thee, Boy !
Thy heart these two weeks has been beating fast
With many hopes ; it should be so—yes—yes—
I knew that thou couldst never have a wish

To leave me, Luke : thou hast been bound to me   400
Only by links of love : when thou art gone,
What will be left to us !—But I forget
My purposes. Lay now the corner-stone,
As I requested ; and hereafter, Luke,
When thou art gone away, should evil men   405
Be thy companions, think of me, my Son,
And of this moment ; hither turn thy thoughts,
And God will strengthen thee : amid all fear
And all temptation, Luke, I pray that thou
May'st bear in mind the life thy Fathers lived,   410
Who, being innocent, did for that cause
Bestir them in good deeds. Now, fare thee well—
When thou return'st, thou in this place wilt see
A work which is not here : a covenant
'Twill be between us ; but, whatever fate   415
Befall thee, I shall love thee to the last,
And bear thy memory with me to the grave.'

   The Shepherd ended here ; and Luke stooped down,
And, as his Father had requested, laid
The first stone of the Sheep-fold. At the sight   420
The old Man's grief broke from him ; to his heart
He pressed his Son, he kissèd him and wept ;
And to the house together they returned.
—Hushed was that House in peace, or seeming peace,
Ere the night fell :—with morrow's dawn the Boy   425
Began his journey, and, when he had reached
The public way, he put on a bold face ;
And all the neighbours, as he passed their doors,
Came forth with wishes and with farewell prayers,
That followed him till he was out of sight.   430

   A good report did from their Kinsman come,
Of Luke and his well-doing : and the Boy

Wrote loving letters, full of wondrous news,
Which, as the Housewife phrased it, were throughout
' The prettiest letters that were ever seen.'   435
Both parents read them with rejoicing hearts.
So, many months passed on : and once again
The Shepherd went about his daily work
With confident and cheerful thoughts ; and now
Sometimes when he could find a leisure hour   440
He to that valley took his way, and there
Wrought at the Sheep-fold. Meantime Luke began
To slacken in his duty ; and, at length,
He in the dissolute city gave himself
To evil courses : ignominy and shame   445
Fell on him, so that he was driven at last
To seek a hiding-place beyond the seas.

   There is a comfort in the strength of love ;
'Twill make a thing endurable, which else
Would overset the brain, or break the heart :   450
I have conversed with more than one who well
Remember the old Man, and what he was
Years after he had heard this heavy news.
His bodily frame had been from youth to age
Of an unusual strength. Among the rocks   455
He went, and still looked up to sun and cloud,
And listened to the wind ; and, as before,
Performed all kinds of labour for his sheep,
And for the land, his small inheritance.
And to that hollow dell from time to time   460
Did he repair, to build the Fold of which
His flock had need. 'Tis not forgotten yet
The pity which was then in every heart
For the old Man—and 'tis believed by all
That many and many a day he thither went,   465
And never lifted up a single stone.

There, by the Sheep-fold, sometimes was he seen
Sitting alone, or with his faithful Dog,
Then old, beside him, lying at his feet.
The length of full seven years, from time to time,   470
He at the building of this Sheep-fold wrought,
And left the work unfinished when he died.
Three years, or little more, did Isabel
Survive her Husband : at her death the estate
Was sold, and went into a stranger's hand.   475
The Cottage which was named the EVENING STAR
Is gone—the ploughshare has been through the ground
On which it stood ; great changes have been wrought
In all the neighbourhood :—yet the oak is left
That grew beside their door ; and the remains   480
Of the unfinished Sheep-fold may be seen
Beside the boisterous brook of Green-head Ghyll.

RESOLUTION

AND

INDEPENDENCE

Composed May 3–July 4, 1802.—Published 1807

I

THERE was a roaring in the wind all night ;
The rain came heavily and fell in floods ;
But now the sun is rising calm and bright ;
The birds are singing in the distant woods ;
Over his own sweet voice the Stock-dove broods ;   5
The Jay makes answer as the Magpie chatters ;
And all the air is filled with pleasant noise of waters.

II

All things that love the sun are out of doors ;
The sky rejoices in the morning's birth ;
The grass is bright with rain-drops ;—on the moors   10
The hare is running races in her mirth ;
And with her feet she from the plashy earth
Raises a mist ; that, glittering in the sun,
Runs with her all the way, wherever she doth run.

III

I was a Traveller then upon the moor ;   15
I saw the hare that raced about with joy ;
I heard the woods and distant waters roar ;
Or heard them not, as happy as a boy :
The pleasant season did my heart employ :
My old remembrances went from me wholly ;   20
And all the ways of men, so vain and melancholy.

IV

But, as it sometimes chanceth, from the might
Of joy in minds that can no further go,
As high as we have mounted in delight
In our dejection do we sink as low;   25
To me that morning did it happen so;
And fears and fancies thick upon me came;
Dim sadness—and blind thoughts, I knew not, nor could
    name.

V

I heard the sky-lark warbling in the sky;
And I bethought me of the playful hare: 30
Even such a happy Child of earth am I;
Even as these blissful creatures do I fare;
Far from the world I walk, and from all care;
But there may come another day to me—
Solitude, pain of heart, distress, and poverty.   35

VI

My whole life I have lived in pleasant thought,
As if life's business were a summer mood;
As if all needful things would come unsought
To genial faith, still rich in genial good;
But how can He expect that others should   40
Build for him, sow for him, and at his call
Love him, who for himself will take no heed at all?

VII

I thought of Chatterton, the marvellous Boy,
The sleepless Soul that perished in his pride;
Of Him who walked in glory and in joy   45
Following his plough, along the mountain-side:
By our own spirits are we deified:
We Poets in our youth begin in gladness;
But thereof come in the end despondency and madness.

VIII

Now, whether it were by peculiar grace,   50
A leading from above, a something given,
Yet it befell that, in this lonely place,
When I with these untoward thoughts had striven,
Beside a pool bare to the eye of heaven
I saw a Man before me unawares: 55
The oldest man he seemed that ever wore grey hairs.

IX

As a huge stone is sometimes seen to lie
Couched on the bald top of an eminence;
Wonder to all who do the same espy,
By what means it could thither come, and whence; 60
So that it seems a thing endued with sense:
Like a sea-beast crawled forth, that on a shelf
Of rock or sand reposeth, there to sun itself;

X

Such seemed this Man, not all alive nor dead,
Nor all asleep—in his extreme old age: 65
His body was bent double, feet and head
Coming together in life's pilgrimage;
As if some dire constraint of pain, or rage
Of sickness felt by him in times long past,
A more than human weight upon his frame had cast. 70

XI

Himself he propped, limbs, body, and pale face,
Upon a long grey staff of shaven wood:
And, still as I drew near with gentle pace,
Upon the margin of that moorish flood
Motionless as a cloud the old Man stood,   75
That heareth not the loud winds when they call;
And moveth all together, if it move at all.

XII

At length, himself unsettling, he the pond
Stirred with his staff, and fixedly did look
Upon the muddy water, which he conned,   80
As if he had been reading in a book:
And now a stranger's privilege I took;
And, drawing to his side, to him did say,
' This morning gives us promise of a glorious day.'

XIII

A gentle answer did the old Man make,   85
In courteous speech which forth he slowly drew:
And him with further words I thus bespake,
' What occupation do you there pursue?
This is a lonesome place for one like you.'
Ere he replied, a flash of mild surprise   90
Broke from the sable orbs of his yet-vivid eyes.

XIV

His words came feebly, from a feeble chest,
But each in solemn order followed each,
With something of a lofty utterance drest—
Choice word and measured phrase, above the reach 95
Of ordinary men; a stately speech;
Such as grave Livers do in Scotland use,
Religious men, who give to God and man their dues.

XV

He told, that to these waters he had come
To gather leeches, being old and poor: 100
Employment hazardous and wearisome!
And he had many hardships to endure:
From pond to pond he roamed, from moor to moor;
Housing, with God's good help, by choice or chance;
And in this way he gained an honest maintenance. 105

XVI

The old Man still stood talking by my side;
But now his voice to me was like a stream
Scarce heard; nor word from word could I divide;
And the whole body of the Man did seem
Like one whom I had met with in a dream;   110
Or like a man from some far region sent,
To give me human strength, by apt admonishment.

XVII

My former thoughts returned: the fear that kills;
And hope that is unwilling to be fed;
Cold, pain, and labour, and all fleshly ills   115
And mighty Poets in their misery dead.
—Perplexed, and longing to be comforted,
My question eagerly did I renew,
' How is it that you live, and what is it you do ? '

XVIII

He with a smile did then his words repeat;   120
And said that, gathering leeches, far and wide
He travelled; stirring thus about his feet
The waters of the pools where they abide.
' Once I could meet with them on every side;
But they have dwindled long by slow decay;   125
Yet still I persevere, and find them where I may.'

XIX

While he was talking thus, the lonely place,
The old Man's shape, and speech—all troubled me:
In my mind's eye I seemed to see him pace
About the weary moors continually,   130
Wandering about alone and silently.
While I these thoughts within myself pursued,
He, having made a pause, the same discourse renewed.

XX

And soon with this he other matter blended,
Cheerfully uttered, with demeanour kind,   135
But stately in the main ; and, when he ended,
I could have laughed myself to scorn to find
In that decrepit Man so firm a mind.
' God,' said I, ' be my help and stay secure :
I'll think of the Leech-gatherer on the lonely moor ! 140

Composed March 26, 1802.—Published 1807

MY heart leaps up when I behold
    A rainbow in the sky :
So was it when my life began ;
So is it now I am a man ;
So be it when I shall grow old,   5
    Or let me die !
The Child is father of the Man ;
And I could wish my days to be
Bound each to each by natural piety.

TO

THE DAISY

Composed 1802.—Published 1807

WITH little here to do or see
Of things that in the great world be,
Daisy ! again I talk to thee,
    For thou art worthy,
Thou unassuming Common-place   5
Of Nature, with that homely face,
And yet with something of a grace
    Which love makes for thee !

Oft on the dappled turf at ease
I sit, and play with similes,   10
Loose types of things through all degrees,
   Thoughts of thy raising :
And many a fond and idle name
I give to thee, for praise or blame,
As is the humour of the game,   15
   While I am gazing.

A nun demure of lowly port ;
Or sprightly maiden, of Love's court,
In thy simplicity the sport
   Of all temptations ;   20
A queen in crown of rubies drest ;
A starveling in a scanty vest ;
Are all, as seems to suit thee best,
   Thy appellations.

A little Cyclops with one eye   25
Staring to threaten and defy,
That thought comes next—and instantly
   The freak is over,
The shape will vanish—and behold
A silver shield with boss of gold,   30
That spreads itself, some faery bold
   In fight to cover !

I see thee glittering from afar—
And then thou art a pretty star ;
Not quite so fair as many are   35
   In heaven above thee !
Yet like a star, with glittering crest,
Self-poised in air thou seem'st to rest ;—
May peace come never to his nest,
   Who shall reprove thee !   40

Bright *Flower!* for by that name at last,
When all my reveries are past,
I call thee, and to that cleave fast,
  Sweet silent creature !
That breath'st with me in sun and air, 45
Do thou, as thou art wont, repair
My heart with gladness, and a share
  Of thy meek nature !

T O

THE CUCKOO

Composed March 23–26, 1802.—Published 1807

O BLITHE New-comer ! I have heard,
I hear thee and rejoice.
O Cuckoo ! shall I call thee Bird,
Or but a wandering Voice ?

While I am lying on the grass 5
Thy twofold shout I hear ;
From hill to hill it seems to pass
At once far off, and near.

Though babbling only to the Vale,
Of sunshine and of flowers, 10
Thou bringest unto me a tale
Of visionary hours.

Thrice welcome, darling of the Spring !
Even yet thou art to me
No bird, but an invisible thing, 15
A voice, a mystery ;

The same whom in my schoolboy days
I listened to; that Cry
Which made me look a thousand ways
In bush, and tree, and sky.   20

To seek thee did I often rove
Through woods and on the green;
And thou wert still a hope, a love;
Still longed for, never seen.

And I can listen to thee yet;   25
Can lie upon the plain
And listen, till I do beget
That golden time again.

O blessèd Bird! the earth we pace
Again appears to be   30
An unsubstantial, faery place;
That is fit home for Thee!

THE

GREEN LINNET

Composed 1803.—Published 1807

BENEATH these fruit-tree boughs that shed
Their snow-white blossoms on my head,
With brightest sunshine round me spread
  Of spring's unclouded weather,
In this sequestered nook how sweet   5
To sit upon my orchard-seat!
And birds and flowers once more to greet
  My last year's friends together.

One have I marked, the happiest guest
In all this covert of the blest: 10
Hail to Thee, far above the rest
  In joy of voice and pinion !
Thou, Linnet ! in thy green array,
Presiding Spirit here to-day,
Dost lead the revels of the May ;   15
  And this is thy dominion.

While birds, and butterflies, and flowers,
Make all one band of paramours,
Thou, ranging up and down the bowers,
  Art sole in thy employment :   20
A Life, a Presence like the Air,
Scattering thy gladness without care,
Too blest with any one to pair ;
  Thyself thy own enjoyment.

Amid yon tuft of hazel trees,   25
That twinkle to the gusty breeze,
Behold him perched in ecstasies,
  Yet seeming still to hover ;
There ! where the flutter of his wings
Upon his back and body flings   30
Shadows and sunny glimmerings,
  That cover him all over.

My dazzled sight he oft deceives,
A Brother of the dancing leaves ;
Then flits, and from the cottage eaves   35
  Pours forth his song in gushes ;
As if by that exulting strain
He mocked and treated with disdain
The voiceless Form he chose to feign,
  While fluttering in the bushes.   40

98

THE
SOLITARY REAPER

Composed between 1803-1805.—Published 1807

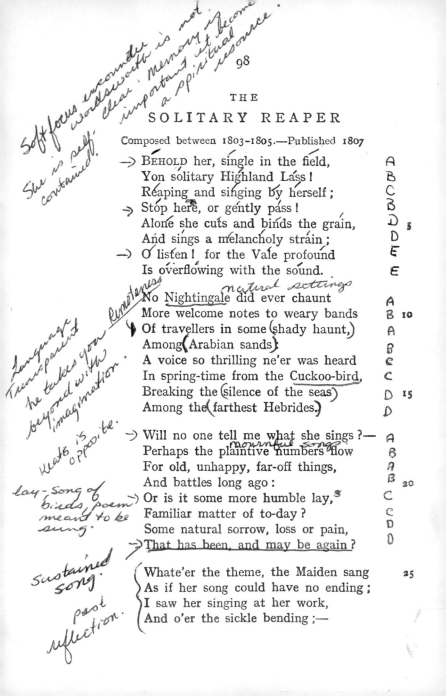

 Behold her, single in the field,   A
 Yon solitary Highland Lass!   B
 Reaping and singing by herself;   C
 Stop here, or gently pass!   B
 Alone she cuts and binds the grain, D 5
 And sings a melancholy strain;   D
 O listen! for the Vale profound   E
 Is overflowing with the sound.   E

 No Nightingale did ever chaunt   A
 More welcome notes to weary bands B 10
 Of travellers in some shady haunt, A
 Among Arabian sands: B
 A voice so thrilling ne'er was heard C
 In spring-time from the Cuckoo-bird, C
 Breaking the silence of the seas   D 15
 Among the farthest Hebrides.   D

 Will no one tell me what she sings?— A
 Perhaps the plaintive numbers flow B
 For old, unhappy, far-off things,   A
 And battles long ago: B 20
 Or is it some more humble lay,   C
 Familiar matter of to-day?   C
 Some natural sorrow, loss or pain, D
 That has been, and may be again?   D

 Whate'er the theme, the Maiden sang   25
 As if her song could have no ending;
 I saw her singing at her work,
 And o'er the sickle bending;—

I listened, motionless and still;
And, as I mounted up the hill,   30
The music in my heart I bore,
Long after it was heard no more.

Composed 1804.—Published 1807

SHE was a Phantom of delight
When first she gleamed upon my sight;
A lovely Apparition, sent
To be a moment's ornament;
Her eyes as stars of Twilight fair;   5
Like Twilight's, too, her dusky hair;
But all things else about her drawn
From May-time and the cheerful Dawn;
A dancing Shape, an Image gay,
To haunt, to startle, and way-lay.   10

I saw her upon nearer view,
A Spirit, yet a Woman too!
Her household motions light and free,
And steps of virgin-liberty;
A countenance in which did meet   15
Sweet records, promises as sweet;
A Creature not too bright or good
For human nature's daily food;
For transient sorrows, simple wiles,
Praise, blame, love, kisses, tears, and smiles. 20

And now I see with eye serene
The very pulse of the machine;
A Being breathing thoughtful breath,
A Traveller between life and death;
The reason firm, the temperate will,   25
Endurance, foresight, strength, and skill:

A perfect Woman, nobly planned,
To warn, to comfort, and command ;
And yet a Spirit still, and bright
With something of angelic light.   30

Joy is important in poet communication.

Composed 1804.—Published 1807_*Joy related to the ideal.*

I WANDERED lonely as a cloud
That floats on high o'er vales and hills,
When all at once I saw a crowd,   *(contrast between ideal & realit*
A host, of golden daffodils ;
Beside the lake, beneath the trees,   5
Fluttering and dancing in the breeze.

vague
↓
ordered

Continuous as the stars that shine
And twinkle on the milky way,
They stretched in never-ending line
Along the margin of a bay :   10
Ten thousand saw I at a glance,
Tossing their heads in sprightly dance.

The waves beside them danced ; but they
Out-did the sparkling waves in glee :
A poet could not but be gay,   15
In such a jocund company :
I gazed—and gazed—but little thought
What wealth the show to me had brought :

Recollection { For oft, when on my couch I lie *(long i)*
In vacant or in pensive mood,   20
They flash upon that inward eye
Which is the bliss of solitude ;
And then my heart with pleasure fills,
And dances with the daffodils.

There is some feelings of

THE

SMALL CELANDINE

Composed 1804.—Published 1807

THERE is a Flower, the lesser Celandine,
That shrinks, like many more, from cold and rain;
And, the first moment that the sun may shine,
Bright as the sun himself, 'tis out again!

When hailstones have been falling, swarm on swarm, 5
Or blasts the green field and the trees distrest,
Oft have I seen it muffled up from harm,
In close self-shelter, like a Thing at rest.

But lately, one rough day, this Flower I passed
And recognised it, though an altered form, 10
Now standing forth an offering to the blast,
And buffeted at will by rain and storm.

I stopped, and said with inly-muttered voice,
' It doth not love the shower, nor seek the cold:
This neither is its courage nor its choice, 15
But its necessity in being old.

' The sunshine may not cheer it, nor the dew;
It cannot help itself in its decay;
Stiff in its members, withered, changed of hue.'
And, in my spleen, I smiled that it was grey. 20

To be a Prodigal's Favourite—then, worse truth,
A Miser's Pensioner—behold our lot!
O Man, that from thy fair and shining youth
Age might but take the things Youth needed not!

H

THE

FRENCH REVOLUTION

AS IT APPEARED TO ENTHUSIASTS AT ITS COMMENCEMENT

Composed 1804.—Published October 26, 1809 (*The Friend*); ed.
1815

Oh! pleasant exercise of hope and joy!
For mighty were the auxiliars which then stood
Upon our side, we who were strong in love!
Bliss was it in that dawn to be alive,
But to be young was very heaven!—Oh! times,   5
In which the meagre, stale, forbidding ways
Of custom, law, and statute, took at once
The attraction of a country in romance!
When Reason seemed the most to assert her rights,
When most intent on making of herself   10
A prime Enchantress—to assist the work
Which then was going forward in her name!
Not favoured spots alone, but the whole earth,
The beauty wore of promise, that which sets
(As at some moment might not be unfelt   15
Among the bowers of paradise itself)
The budding rose above the rose full blown.
What temper at the prospect did not wake
To happiness unthought of? The inert
Were roused, and lively natures rapt away!   20
They who had fed their childhood upon dreams,
The playfellows of fancy, who had made
All powers of swiftness, subtilty, and strength
Their ministers,—who in lordly wise had stirred
Among the grandest objects of the sense,   25
And dealt with whatsoever they found there

As if they had within some lurking right
To wield it ;—they, too, who, of gentle mood,
Had watched all gentle motions, and to these
Had fitted their own thoughts, schemers more mild, 30
And in the region of their peaceful selves ;—
Now was it that both found, the meek and lofty
Did both find, helpers to their heart's desire,
And stuff at hand, plastic as they could wish ;
Were called upon to exercise their skill,   35
Not in Utopia, subterranean fields,
Or some secreted island, Heaven knows where !
But in the very world, which is the world
Of all of us,—the place where in the end
We find our happiness, or not at all !   40

ODE

TO DUTY

Composed 1805.—Published 1807

STERN Daughter of the Voice of God !
O Duty ! if that name thou love
Who art a light to guide, a rod
To check the erring, and reprove ;
Thou, who art victory and law   5
When empty terrors overawe ;
From vain temptations dost set free ;
And calm'st the weary strife of frail humanity !

There are who ask not if thine eye
Be on them ; who, in love and truth,   10
Where no misgiving is, rely
Upon the genial sense of youth :

Glad Hearts! without reproach or blot;
Who do thy work, and know it not:
Oh! if through confidence misplaced 15
They fail, thy saving arms, dread Power! around them cast.

Serene will be our days and bright,
And happy will our nature be,
When love is an unerring light,
And joy its own security. 20
And they a blissful course may hold
Even now, who, not unwisely bold,
Live in the spirit of this creed;
Yet seek thy firm support, according to their need.

I, loving freedom, and untried; *can't trust his own lines any more.*
No sport of every random gust,
Yet being to myself a guide,
Too blindly have reposed my trust;
And oft, when in my heart was heard
Thy timely mandate, I deferred 30
The task, in smoother walks to stray;
But thee I now would serve more strictly, if I may.

Through no disturbance of my soul,
Or strong compunction in me wrought,
I supplicate for thy control; 35
But in the quietness of thought:
Still looking for ideal Me this unchartered freedom tires;
I feel the weight of chance-desires:
My hopes no more must change their name,
I long for a repose that ever is the same. 40

God - Stern Lawgiver! yet thou dost wear
The Godhead's most benignant grace;
Nor know we anything so fair
As is the smile upon thy face:

Still awsome + powerful but now seen as the church sees him, not set in nature

Flowers laugh before thee on their beds 45
And fragrance in thy footing treads;
Thou dost preserve the stars from wrong;
And the most ancient heavens, through Thee, are fresh
    and strong.

To humbler functions, awful Power!
I call thee: I myself commend 50
Unto thy guidance from this hour;
Oh, let my weakness have an end!
Give unto me, made lowly wise,
The spirit of self-sacrifice;
The confidence of reason give; 55
And in the light of truth thy Bondman let me live!

ELEGIAC STANZAS

[handwritten: p 100. Same quality as picture of daffodils (Platonic)]

SUGGESTED BY A PICTURE OF PEELE CASTLE, IN A STORM,

PAINTED BY SIR GEORGE BEAUMONT

Composed 1805.—Published 1807

I was thy neighbour once, thou rugged Pile!
Four summer weeks I dwelt in sight of thee:
I saw thee every day; and all the while
Thy Form was sleeping on a glassy sea.

[handwritten: Represents actual circumstances of his brother's death.]

So pure the sky, so quiet was the air!
So like, so very like, was day to day! 5
Whene'er I looked, thy Image still was there;
It trembled, but it never passed away.

How perfect was the calm! it seemed no sleep;
No mood, which season takes away, or brings:
I could have fancied that the mighty Deep 10
Was even the gentlest of all gentle Things.

[handwritten: depth of poet's vision]

[handwritten: He sees himself painting picture of what's in his mind.]

Ah! THEN, if mine had been the Painter's hand,
To express what then I saw; and add the gleam,
The light that never was, on sea or land, 15
The consecration, and the Poet's dream;

I would have planted thee, thou hoary Pile
Amid a world how different from this!
Beside a sea that could not cease to smile;
On tranquil land, beneath a sky of bliss. 20

Thou shouldst have seemed a treasure-house divine
Of peaceful years; a chronicle of heaven;—
Of all the sunbeams that did ever shine
The very sweetest had to thee been given.

A Picture had it been of lasting ease, 25
Elysian quiet, without toil or strife;
No motion but the moving tide, a breeze,
Or merely silent Nature's breathing life.

Such, in the fond illusion of my heart,
Such Picture would I at that time have made: 30
And seen the soul of truth in every part,
A steadfast peace that might not be betrayed.

So once it would have been,—'tis so no more;
I have submitted to a new control:
A power is gone, which nothing can restore: 35
A deep distress hath humanised my Soul.

Not for a moment could I now behold
A smiling sea, and be what I have been:
The feeling of my loss will ne'er be old;
This, which I know, I speak with mind serene. 40

Beaumont is important to Wordsworth because he is leading him back into the church.

107 *Calls on the painter, not Dorothy.*

Then, Beaumont, Friend! who would have been the
    Friend.
If he had lived, of Him whom I deplore,
This work of thine I blame not, but commend:
This sea in anger, and that dismal shore.

O 'tis a passionate Work!—yet wise and well,   45
Well chosen is the spirit that is here;
That Hulk which labours in the deadly swell,
This rueful sky, this pageantry of fear! *a colourful clothing*
(yet awe inspiring & terrifying)

And this huge Castle, standing here sublime,
I love to see the look with which it braves, *He enjoys the*
Cased in the unfeeling armour of old time,   *picture.*   50
The lightning, the fierce wind, and trampling waves.

Farewell, farewell the heart that lives alone,
Housed in a dream, at distance from the Kind!
Such happiness, wherever it be known,   55
Is to be pitied; for 'tis surely blind.

But welcome fortitude, and patient cheer,
And frequent sights of what is to be borne!
Such sights, or worse, as are before me here.—
Not without hope we suffer and we mourn.   60

fond illusion.

thr' the picture there is the power to record events.

Traditional lineaments of Christian God are now beginning to appear.

(left margin: farewell to his earlier state of mind.)

CHARACTER

OF THE

HAPPY WARRIOR

Composed December 1805 or January 1806.—Published 1807

Who is the happy Warrior? Who is he
That every man in arms should wish to be?
—It is the generous Spirit, who, when brought
Among the tasks of real life, hath wrought
Upon the plan that pleased his boyish thought: 5
Whose high endeavours are an inward light
That makes the path before him always bright:
Who, with a natural instinct to discern
What knowledge can perform, is diligent to learn;
Abides by this resolve, and stops not there,   10
But makes his moral being his prime care;
Who, doomed to go in company with Pain,
And Fear, and Bloodshed, miserable train!
Turns his necessity to glorious gain;
In face of these doth exercise a power   15
Which is our human nature's highest dower;
Controls them and subdues, transmutes, bereaves
Of their bad influence, and their good receives:
By objects, which might force the soul to abate
Her feeling, rendered more compassionate;   20
Is placable—because occasions rise
So often that demand such sacrifice;
More skilful in self-knowledge, even more pure,
As tempted more; more able to endure,
As more exposed to suffering and distress;   25
Thence, also, more alive to tenderness.

—'Tis he whose law is reason ; who depends
Upon that law as on the best of friends ;
Whence, in a state where men are tempted still
To evil for a guard against worse ill,   30
And what in quality or act is best
Doth seldom on a right foundation rest,
He labours good on good to fix, and owes
To virtue every triumph that he knows :
—Who, if he rise to station of command,   35
Rises by open means ; and there will stand
On honourable terms, or else retire,
And in himself possess his own desire ;
Who comprehends his trust, and to the same
Keeps faithful with a singleness of aim ;   40
And therefore does not stoop, nor lie in wait
For wealth, or honours, or for worldly state ;
Whom they must follow ; on whose head must fall,
Like showers of manna, if they come at all :
Whose powers shed round him in the common strife, 45
Or mild concerns of ordinary life,
A constant influence, a peculiar grace ;
But who, if he be called upon to face
Some awful moment to which Heaven has joined
Great issues, good or bad for human kind,   50
Is happy as a Lover ; and attired
With sudden brightness, like a Man inspired ;
And, through the heat of conflict, keeps the law
In calmness made, and sees what he foresaw ;
Or if an unexpected call succeed,   55
Come when it will, is equal to the need :
—He who, though thus endued as with a sense
And faculty for storm and turbulence,
Is yet a Soul whose master-bias leans
To homefelt pleasures and to gentle scenes ;   60
Sweet images ! which, wheresoe'er he be,

Are at his heart ; and such fidelity
It is his darling passion to approve ;
More brave for this, that he hath much to love :——
'Tis, finally, the Man, who, lifted high,   65
Conspicuous object in a Nation's eye,
Or left unthought-of in obscurity,—
Who, with a toward or untoward lot,
Prosperous or adverse, to his wish or not—
Plays, in the many games of life, that one   70
Where what he most doth value must be won :
Whom neither shape of danger can dismay,
Nor thought of tender happiness betray ;
Who, not content that former worth stand fast,
Looks forward, persevering to the last,   75
From well to better, daily self-surpast :
Who, whether praise of him must walk the earth
For ever, and to noble deeds give birth,
Or he must fall, to sleep without his fame,
And leave a dead unprofitable name—   80
Finds comfort in himself and in his cause ;
And, while the mortal mist is gathering, draws
His breath in confidence of Heaven's applause :
This is the happy Warrior ; this is He
That every Man in arms should wish to be.   85

LINES

Composed at Grasmere, during a walk one Evening, after a stormy
day, the Author having just read in a Newspaper that the
dissolution of Mr. Fox was hourly expected.

Composed September 1806.—Published 1807

LOUD is the Vale ! the Voice is up
With which she speaks when storms are gone,
A mighty unison of streams !
Of all her Voices, One !

Loud is the Vale ;—this inland Depth   5
In peace is roaring like the Sea ;
Yon star upon the mountain-top
Is listening quietly.

Sad was I, even to pain deprest,
Importunate and heavy load !   10
The Comforter hath found me here,
Upon this lonely road ;

And many thousands now are sad—
Wait the fulfilment of their fear ;
For he must die who is their stay,   15
Their glory disappear.

A Power is passing from the earth
To breathless Nature's dark abyss ;
But when the great and good depart
What is it more than this—   20

That Man. who is from God sent forth,
Doth yet again to God return ?—
Such ebb and flow must ever be,
Then wherefore should we mourn ?

*Structural means to bring unity
to this poem.*

ODE

INTIMATIONS OF IMMORTALITY FROM RECOLLECTIONS OF EARLY CHILDHOOD

Composed 1802-1806.—Published 1807

I

THERE was a time when meadow, grove, and stream,   A
The earth, and every common sight,   B
    To me did seem   A
   Apparelled in celestial light,   B
The glory and the freshness of a dream.   5   A

112

It is not now as it hath been of yore :—
    Turn wheresoe'er I may,
    By night or day,
The things which I have seen I now can see no more.

II

    The Rainbow comes and goes,
    And lovely is the Rose,
    The Moon doth with delight
Look round her when the heavens are bare,
    Waters on a starry night
    Are beautiful and fair ;
The sunshine is a glorious birth ;
But yet I know, where'er I go,
That there hath past away a glory from the earth.

III

Now, while the birds thus sing a joyous song,
    And while the young lambs bound
    As to the tabor's sound,
To me alone there came a thought of grief :
A timely utterance gave that thought relief,
    And I again am strong :
The cataracts blow their trumpets from the steep ;
No more shall grief of mine the season wrong ;
I hear the Echoes through the mountains throng,
The Winds come to me from the fields of sleep,
    And all the earth is gay ;
    Land and sea
    Give themselves up to jollity,
    And with the heart of May
    Doth every Beast keep holiday ;—
    Thou Child of Joy,
Shout round me, let me hear thy shouts, thou happy
    Shepherd-boy !

IV

Ye blessèd Creatures, I have heard the call
  Ye to each other make ; I see
The heavens laugh with you in your jubilee ;
  My heart is at your festival,
    My head hath its coronal,   40
The fulness of your bliss, I feel—I feel it all.
    Oh evil day ! if I were sullen
    While Earth herself is adorning,
      This sweet May-morning,
    And the Children are culling   45
      On every side,
    In a thousand valleys far and wide,
    Fresh flowers ; while the sun shines warm,
And the Babe leaps up on his Mother's arm :—
    I hear, I hear, with joy I hear !   50
    —But there 's a Tree, of many, one,
A single Field which I have looked upon,
Both of them speak of something that is gone :
    The Pansy at my feet
    Doth the same tale repeat :   55
Whither is fled the visionary gleam ?
Where is it now, the glory and the dream ?

V

Our birth is but a sleep and a forgetting :
The Soul that rises with us, our life's Star,
    Hath had elsewhere its setting,   60
    And cometh from afar :
    Not in entire forgetfulness,
    And not in utter nakedness,
But trailing clouds of glory do we come
    From God, who is our home :   65
Heaven lies about us in our infancy !
Shades of the prison-house begin to close
    Upon the growing Boy,

But He beholds the light, and whence it flows,
　　　He sees it in his joy ;　　　　　　　　　*70*
The Youth, who daily farther from the east
　　　Must travel, still is Nature's Priest,
　　　　　And by the vision splendid
　　　　　Is on his way attended :
At length the Man perceives it die away,　　　*75*
And fade into the light of common day.

VI

Earth fills her lap with pleasures of her own ;
Yearnings she hath in her own natural kind,
And, even with something of a Mother's mind,
　　　　　And no unworthy aim,　　　　　　*80*
　　　The homely Nurse doth all she can
To make her Foster-child, her Inmate Man,
　　　Forget the glories he hath known,
And that imperial palace whence he came.

VII

Behold the Child among his new-born blisses,　*85*
A six years' Darling of a pigmy size !
See, where 'mid work of his own hand he lies,
Fretted by sallies of his mother's kisses,
With light upon him from his father's eyes !
See, at his feet, some little plan or chart,　　*90*
Some fragment from his dream of human life,
Shaped by himself with newly-learned art ;
　　　　A wedding or a festival,
　　　　A mourning or a funeral ;
　　　　　And this hath now his heart,　　*95*
　　　　And unto this he frames his song :
　　　　　Then will he fit his tongue
To dialogues of business, love, or strife ;
　　　　But it will not be long

Ere this be thrown aside,   100
    And with new joy and pride
The little Actor cons another part ;
Filling from time to time his 'humorous stage '
With all the Persons, down to palsied Age,
That Life brings with her in her equipage ;   105
    As if his whole vocation
    Were endless imitation.

VIII

Thou, whose exterior semblance doth belie
    Thy Soul's immensity ;
Thou best Philosopher, who yet dost keep   110
Thy heritage, thou Eye among the blind,
That, deaf and silent, read'st the eternal deep,
Haunted for ever by the eternal mind,
    Mighty Prophet ! Seer blest !
    On whom those truths do rest,   115
Which we are toiling all our lives to find,
In darkness lost, the darkness of the grave ;
Thou, over whom thy Immortality
Broods like the Day, a Master o'er a Slave,
A Presence which is not to be put by ;   120
    [To whom the grave
Is but a lonely bed without the sense or sight
    Of day or the warm light,
A place of thought where we in waiting lie ;]
Thou little Child, yet glorious in the might   125
Of heaven-born freedom on thy being's height,
Why with such earnest pains dost thou provoke
The years to bring the inevitable yoke,
Thus blindly with thy blessedness at strife ?
Full soon thy Soul shall have her earthly freight, 130
And custom lie upon thee with a weight,
Heavy as frost, and deep almost as life !

IX

O joy ! that in our embers
Is something that doth live,
That nature yet remembers   135
What was so fugitive !
The thought of our past years in me doth breed
Perpetual benediction : not indeed
For that which is most worthy to be blest ;
Delight and liberty, the simple creed   140
Of Childhood, whether busy or at rest,
With new-fledged hope still fluttering in his breast :—
        Not for these I raise
        The song of thanks and praise ;
        But for those obstinate questionings   145
        Of sense and outward things,
        Fallings from us, vanishings ;
        Blank misgivings of a Creature
Moving about in worlds not realised,
High instincts before which our mortal Nature   150
Did tremble like a guilty Thing surprised :
        But for those first affections,
        Those shadowy recollections,
        Which, be they what they may,
Are yet the fountain-light of all our day,   155
Are yet a master-light of all our seeing ;
        Uphold us, cherish, and have power to make
Our noisy years seem moments in the being
Of the eternal Silence : truths that wake,
        To perish never :   160
Which neither listlessness, nor mad endeavour,
        Nor Man nor Boy,
Nor all that is at enmity with joy,
Can utterly abolish or destroy !
        Hence in a season of calm weather   165

Though inland far we be,
Our Souls have sight of that immortal sea
   Which brought us hither,
   Can in a moment travel thither,
And see the Children sport upon the shore,   170
And hear the mighty waters rolling evermore.

X

Then sing, ye Birds, sing, sing a joyous song!
   And let the young Lambs bound
   As to the tabor's sound!
We in thought will join your throng,   175
   Ye that pipe and ye that play,
   Ye that through your hearts to-day
   Feel the gladness of the May!
What though the radiance which was once so bright
Be now for ever taken from my sight,   180
   Though nothing can bring back the hour
Of splendour in the grass, of glory in the flower;
   We will grieve not, rather find
   Strength in what remains behind;
   In the primal sympathy   185
   Which having been must ever be;
   In the soothing thoughts that spring
   Out of human suffering;
   In the faith that looks through death,
In years that bring the philosophic mind.   190

XI

And O, ye Fountains, Meadows, Hills, and Groves,
Forebode not any severing of our loves!
Yet in my heart of hearts I feel your might;
I only have relinquished one delight
To live beneath your more habitual sway.   195
I love the Brooks which down their channels fret.

Even more than when I tripped lightly as they;
The innocent brightness of a new-born Day
      Is lovely yet;
The Clouds that gather round the setting sun   200
Do take a sober colouring from an eye
That hath kept watch o'er man's mortality;
Another race hath been, and other palms are won.
Thanks to the human heart by which we live,
Thanks to its tenderness, its joys, and fears,   205
To me the meanest flower that blows can give
Thoughts that do often lie too deep for tears.

SONG

AT THE

FEAST OF BROUGHAM CASTLE

UPON THE RESTORATION OF LORD CLIFFORD, THE
SHEPHERD, TO THE ESTATES AND HONOURS
OF HIS ANCESTORS

Composed 1807.—Published 1807

HIGH in the breathless Hall the Minstrel sate,
And Emont's murmur mingled with the Song.—
The words of ancient time I thus translate,
A festal strain that hath been silent long:—

  ' From town to town, from tower to tower,   5
The red rose is a gladsome flower.
Her thirty years of winter past,
The red rose is revived at last;
She lifts her head for endless spring,
For everlasting blossoming: 10
Both roses flourish, red and white:
In love and sisterly delight

The two that were at strife are blended,
And all old troubles now are ended.—
Joy ! joy to both ! but most to her   15
Who is the flower of Lancaster !
Behold her how She smiles to-day
On this great throng, this bright array !
Fair greeting doth she send to all
From every corner of the hall ;   20
But chiefly from above the board
Where sits in state our rightful Lord,
A Clifford to his own restored !

  ' They came with banner, spear, and shield ;
And it was proved in Bosworth-field.   25
Not long the Avenger was withstood—
Earth helped him with the cry of blood :
St. George was for us, and the might
Of blessed Angels crowned the right.
Loud voice the Land has uttered forth,   30
We loudest in the faithful north :
Our fields rejoice, our mountains ring,
Our streams proclaim a welcoming ;
Our strong-abodes and castles see
The glory of their loyalty.   35

  ' How glad is Skipton at this hour—
Though lonely, a deserted Tower ;
Knight, squire, and yeoman, page and groom :
We have them at the feast of Brough'm.
How glad Pendragon—though the sleep   40
Of years be on her !—She shall reap
A taste of this great pleasure, viewing
As in a dream her own renewing.
Rejoiced is Brough, right glad, I deem,
Beside her little humble stream ;   45

And she that keepeth watch and ward
Her statelier Eden's course to guard ;
They both are happy at this hour,
Though each is but a lonely Tower :—
But here is perfect joy and pride   50
For one fair House by Emont's side,
This day, distinguished without peer,
To see her Master and to cheer—
Him, and his Lady-mother dear !

    ' Oh ! it was a time forlorn   55
When the fatherless was born—
Give her wings that she may fly,
Or she sees her infant die !
Swords that are with slaughter wild
Hunt the Mother and the Child.   60
Who will take them from the light ?
—Yonder is a man in sight—
Yonder is a house—but where ?
No, they must not enter there.
To the caves, and to the brooks,   65
To the clouds of heaven she looks ;
She is speechless, but her eyes
Pray in ghostly agonies.
Blissful Mary, Mother mild,
Maid and Mother undefiled,   70
Save a Mother and her Child !

    ' Now Who is he that bounds with joy
On Carrock's side, a Shepherd-boy ?
No thoughts hath he but thoughts that pass
Light as the wind along the grass.   75
Can this be He who hither came
In secret, like a smothered flame ?
O'er whom such thankful tears were shed
For shelter, and a poor man's bread !

God loves the Child ; and God hath willed   80
That those dear words should be fulfilled,
The Lady's words, when forced away
The last she to her Babe did say :
" My own, my own, thy Fellow-guest
I may not be ; but rest thee, rest,   85
For lowly shepherd's life is best ! "

  ' Alas ! when evil men are strong
No life is good, no pleasure long.
The Boy must part from Mosedale's groves,
And leave Blencathara's rugged coves,   90
And quit the flowers that summer brings
To Glenderamakin's lofty springs ;
Must vanish, and his careless cheer
Be turned to heaviness and fear.
—Give Sir Lancelot Threlkeld praise !   95
Hear it, good man, old in days !
Thou tree of covert and of rest
For this young Bird that is distrest ;
Among thy branches safe he lay,
And he was free to sport and play,   100
When falcons were abroad for prey.

  ' A recreant harp, that sings of fear
And heaviness in Clifford's ear !
I said, when evil men are strong,
No life is good, no pleasure long,   105
A weak and cowardly untruth !
Our Clifford was a happy Youth,
And thankful through a weary time,
That brought him up to manhood's prime.
—Again he wanders forth at will,   110
And tends a flock from hill to hill :
His garb is humble ; ne'er was seen
Such garb with such a noble mien ;

Among the shepherd-grooms no mate
Hath he, a Child of strength and state ! 115
Yet lacks not friends for simple glee,
Nor yet for higher sympathy.
To his side the fallow-deer
Came, and rested without fear ;
The eagle, lord of land and sea, 120
Stooped down to pay him fealty ;
And both the undying fish that swim
Through Bowscale-tarn did wait on him ;
The pair were servants of his eye
In their immortality ; 125
And glancing, gleaming, dark or bright,
Moved to and fro, for his delight.
He knew the rocks which Angels haunt
Upon the mountains visitant ;
He hath kenned them taking wing : 130
And into caves where Faeries sing
He hath entered ; and been told
By Voices how men lived of old.
Among the heavens his eye can see
The face of thing that is to be ; 135
And, if that men report him right,
His tongue could whisper words of might.
—Now another day is come,
Fitter hope, and nobler doom ;
He hath thrown aside his crook, 140
And hath buried deep his book ;
Armour rusting in his halls
On the blood of Clifford calls ;—
" Quell the Scot," exclaims the Lance—
Bear me to the heart of France, 145
Is the longing of the Shield -
Tell thy name, thou trembling Field ;

Field of death, where'er thou be,
Groan thou with our victory !
Happy day, and mighty hour,   150
When our Shepherd in his power,
Mailed and horsed, with lance and sword,
To his ancestors restored
Like a re-appearing Star,
Like a glory from afar,   155
First shall head the flock of war ! '

Alas ! the impassioned minstrel did not know
How, by Heaven's grace, this Clifford's heart was framed :
How he, long forced in humble walks to go,
Was softened into feeling, soothed, and tamed.   160

Love had he found in huts where poor men lie ;
His daily teachers had been woods and rills,
The silence that is in the starry sky,
The sleep that is among the lonely hills.

In him the savage virtue of the Race,   165
Revenge, and all ferocious thoughts were dead :
Nor did he change ; but kept in lofty place
The wisdom which adversity had bred.

Glad were the vales, and every cottage-hearth ;
The Shepherd-lord was honoured more and more ;   170
And, ages after he was laid in earth,
' The good Lord Clifford ' was the name he bore.

LAODAMIA

Composed 1814.—Published 1815

' WITH sacrifice before the rising morn
Vows have I made by fruitless hope inspired ;
And from the infernal Gods, 'mid shades forlorn
Of night, my slaughtered Lord have I required :
Celestial pity I again implore ;—   5
Restore him to my sight—great Jove, restore ! '

So speaking, and by fervent love endowed
With faith, the Suppliant heavenward lifts her hands ;
While, like the sun emerging from a cloud,
Her countenance brightens—and her eye expands ;   10
Her bosom heaves and spreads, her stature grows ;
And she expects the issue in repose.

O terror ! what hath she perceived ?—O joy !
What doth she look on ?—whom doth she behold ?
Her Hero slain upon the beach of Troy ?   15
His vital presence ? his corporeal mould ?
It is—if sense deceive her not—'tis He !
And a God leads him, wingèd Mercury !

Mild Hermes spake—and touched her with his wand
That calms all fear ; ' Such grace hath crowned thy prayer,
Laodamía ! that at Jove's command   21
Thy Husband walks the paths of upper air :
He comes to tarry with thee three hours' space ;
Accept the gift, behold him face to face ! '

Forth sprang the impassioned Queen her Lord to clasp ;
Again that consummation she essayed ;   26
But unsubstantial Form eludes her grasp
As often as that eager grasp was made.

The Phantom parts—but parts to re-unite,
And re-assume his place before her sight.   30

' Protesiláus, lo ! thy guide is gone !
Confirm, I pray, the vision with thy voice :
This is our palace,—yonder is thy throne ;
Speak, and the floor thou tread'st on will rejoice.
Not to appal me have the gods bestowed   35
This precious boon ; and blest a sad abode.'

' Great Jove, Laodamía ! doth not leave
His gifts imperfect :—Spectre though I be,
I am not sent to scare thee or deceive ;
But in reward of thy fidelity.   40
And something also did my worth obtain ;
For fearless virtue bringeth boundless gain.

' Thou knowest, the Delphic oracle foretold
That the first Greek who touched the Trojan strand
Should die ; but me the threat could not withhold : 45
A generous cause a victim did demand ;
And forth I leapt upon the sandy plain ;
A self-devoted chief—by Hector slain.'

' Supreme of Heroes—bravest, noblest, best !
Thy matchless courage I bewail no more,   50
Which then, when tens of thousands were deprest
By doubt, propelled thee to the fatal shore ;
Thou found'st—and I forgive thee—here thou art—
A nobler counsellor than my poor heart.

' But thou, though capable of sternest deed,   55
Wert kind as resolute, and good as brave ;
And he, whose power restores thee, hath decreed
Thou shouldst elude the malice of the grave :
Redundant are thy locks, thy lips as fair
As when their breath enriched Thessalian air.   60

' No Spectre greets me,—no vain Shadow this ;
Come, blooming Hero, place thee by my side !
Give, on this well-known couch, one nuptial kiss
To me, this day, a second time thy bride ! '
Jove frowned in heaven : the conscious Parcæ threw   65
Upon those roseate lips a Stygian hue.

' This visage tells thee that my doom is past :
Nor should the change be mourned, even if the joys
Of sense were able to return as fast
And surely as they vanish.   Earth destroys   70
Those raptures duly—Erebus disdains :
Calm pleasures there abide—majestic pains.

' Be taught, O faithful Consort, to control
Rebellious passion : for the Gods approve
The depth, and not the tumult, of the soul ;   75
A fervent, not ungovernable, love.
Thy transports moderate ; and meekly mourn
When I depart, for brief is my sojourn— '

' Ah wherefore ?—Did not Hercules by force
Wrest from the guardian Monster of the tomb   80
Alcestis, a reanimated corse,
Given back to dwell on earth in vernal bloom ?
Medea's spells dispersed the weight of years,
And Æson stood a youth 'mid youthful peers.

' The Gods to us are merciful—and they   85
Yet further may relent : for mightier far
Than strength of nerve and sinew, or the sway
Of magic potent over sun and star,
Is love, though oft to agony distrest,
And though his favourite seat be feeble woman's breast.   90

'But if thou goest, I follow—' 'Peace!' he said,—
She looked upon him and was calmed and cheered;
The ghastly colour from his lips had fled;
In his deportment, shape, and mien, appeared
Elysian beauty, melancholy grace,   95
Brought from a pensive though a happy place.

He spake of love, such love as Spirits feel
In worlds whose course is equable and pure;
No fears to beat away—no strife to heal—
The past unsighed for, and the future sure;   100
Spake of heroic arts in graver mood
Revived, with finer harmony pursued;

Of all that is most beauteous—imaged there
In happier beauty; more pellucid streams,
An ampler ether, a diviner air,   105
And fields invested with purpureal gleams;
Climes which the sun, who sheds the brightest day
Earth knows, is all unworthy to survey.

Yet there the Soul shall enter which hath earned
That privilege by virtue.—'Ill,' said he,   110
'The end of man's existence I discerned,
Who from ignoble games and revelry
Could draw, when we had parted, vain delight,
While tears were thy best pastime, day and night;

'And while my youthful peers before my eyes   115
(Each hero following his peculiar bent)
Prepared themselves for glorious enterprise
By martial sports,—or, seated in the tent,
Chieftains and kings in council were detained;
What time the fleet at Aulis lay enchained.   120

'The wished-for wind was given :—I then revolved
The oracle, upon the silent sea ;
And, if no worthier led the way, resolved
That, of a thousand vessels, mine should be
The foremost prow in pressing to the strand,—   125
Mine the first blood that tinged the Trojan sand.

'Yet bitter, oft-times bitter, was the pang
When of thy loss I thought, belovèd Wife !
On thee too fondly did my memory hang,
And on the joys we shared in mortal life,—   130
The paths which we had trod—these fountains, flowers ;
My new-planned cities, and unfinished towers.

'But should suspense permit the Foe to cry,
"Behold they tremble !—haughty their array,
Yet of their number no one dares to die ? "   135
In soul I swept the indignity away :
Old frailties then recurred :—but lofty thought,
In act embodied, my deliverance wrought.

'And Thou, though strong in love, art all too weak
In reason, in self-government too slow ;   140
I counsel thee by fortitude to seek
Our blest re-union in the shades below.
The invisible world with thee hath sympathised ;
Be thy affections raised and solemnised.

'Learn, by a mortal yearning, to ascend—   145
Seeking a higher object. Love was given,
Encouraged, sanctioned, chiefly for that end ;
For this the passion to excess was driven—
That self might be annulled : her bondage prove
The fetters of a dream opposed to love.'—   150

Aloud she shrieked ! for Hermes reappears !
Round the dear Shade she would have clung—'tis vain :
The hours are past—too brief had they been years ;
And him no mortal effort can detain :
Swift, toward the realms that know not earthly day,   155
He through the portal takes his silent way,
And on the palace-floor a lifeless corse She lay.

Thus, all in vain exhorted and reproved,
She perished ; and, as for a wilful crime,
By the just Gods whom no weak pity moved,   160
Was doomed to wear out her appointed time,
Apart from happy Ghosts, that gather flowers
Of blissful quiet 'mid unfading bowers.

—Yet tears to human suffering are due ;
And mortal hopes defeated and o'erthrown   165
Are mourned by man, and not by man alone,
As fondly he believes.—Upon the side
Of Hellespont (such faith was entertained)
A knot of spiry trees for ages grew
From out the tomb of him for whom she died ;   170
And ever, when such stature they had gained
That Ilium's walls were subject to their view,
The trees' tall summits withered at the sight ;
A constant interchange of growth and blight ![1]

[1] For the account of these long-lived trees, see Pliny's *Natural History*, lib. xvi. cap. 44 ; and for the features in the character of Protesilaus, see the *Iphigenia in Aulis* of Euripides. Virgil places the Shade of Laodamia in a mournful region, among unhappy Lovers,

————His Laodamia

It comes.————

AN EVENING OF EXTRAORDINARY SPLENDOUR AND BEAUTY

Composed 1818.—Published 1820

I

HAD this effulgence disappeared
With flying haste, I might have sent,
Among the speechless clouds, a look
Of blank astonishment ;
But 'tis endued with power to stay,⁣   5
And sanctify one closing day,
That frail Mortality may see—
What is ?—ah no, but what *can* be !
Time was when field and watery cove
With modulated echoes rang,⁣   10
While choirs of fervent Angels sang
Their vespers in the grove ;
Or, crowning, star-like, each some sovereign height,
Warbled, for heaven above and earth below,
Strains suitable to both.—Such holy rite,⁣   15
Methinks, if audibly repeated now
From hill or valley, could not move
Sublimer transport, purer love,
Than doth this silent spectacle—the gleam—
The shadow—and the peace supreme !⁣   20

II

No sound is uttered,—but a deep
And solemn harmony pervades
The hollow vale from steep to steep,
And penetrates the glades.
Far-distant images draw nigh,⁣   25
Called forth by wondrous potency

Of beamy radiance, that imbues
Whate'er it strikes with gem-like hues !
In vision exquisitely clear,
Herds range along the mountain side ;   30
And glistening antlers are descried ;
And gilded flocks appear.
Thine is the tranquil hour, purpureal Eve !
But long as god-like wish, or hope divine,
Informs my spirit, ne'er can I believe   35
That this magnificence is wholly thine !
—From worlds not quickened by the sun
A portion of the gift is won ;
An intermingling of Heaven's pomp is spread
On ground which British shepherds tread !   40

III

And if there be whom broken ties
Afflict, or injuries assail,
Yon hazy ridges to their eyes
Present a glorious scale,
Climbing suffused with sunny air,   45
To stop—no record hath told where !
And tempting Fancy to ascend,
And with immortal Spirits blend !
—Wings at my shoulders seem to play ;
But, rooted here, I stand and gaze   50
On those bright steps that heavenward raise
Their practicable way.
Come forth, ye drooping old men, look abroad,
And see to what fair countries ye are bound !
And if some traveller, weary of his road,   55
Hath slept since noon-tide on the grassy ground,
Ye Genii ! to his covert speed ;
And wake him with such gentle heed
As may attune his soul to meet the dower
Bestowed on this transcendent hour !   60

IV

Such hues from their celestial Urn
Were wont to stream before mine eye,
Where'er it wandered in the morn
Of blissful infancy.
This glimpse of glory, why renewed ?   65
Nay, rather speak with gratitude ;
For, if a vestige of those gleams
Survived, 'twas only in my dreams.
Dread Power ! whom peace and calmness serve
No less than Nature's threatening voice,   70
If aught unworthy be my choice,
From THEE if I would swerve ;
Oh, let Thy grace remind me of the light
Full early lost, and fruitlessly deplored ;
Which, at this moment, on my waking sight   75
Appears to shine, by miracle restored ;
My soul, though yet confined to earth,
Rejoices in a second birth !
—'Tis past, the visionary splendour fades ;
And night approaches with her shades.   80

TO A SKYLARK
Composed 1825.—Published 1827
ETHEREAL minstrel ! pilgrim of the sky !
Dost thou despise the earth where cares abound ?
Or, while the wings aspire, are heart and eye
Both with thy nest upon the dewy ground ?
Thy nest which thou canst drop into at will,   5
Those quivering wings composed, that music still !

Leave to the nightingale her shady wood ;
A privacy of glorious light is thine ;
Whence thou dost pour upon the world a flood
Of harmony, with instinct more divine ;   10
Type of the wise who soar, but never roam ;
True to the kindred points of Heaven and Home !

YARROW REVISITED

The following Stanzas are a memorial of a day passed with Sir
Walter Scott and other Friends visiting the Banks of the
Yarrow under his guidance, immediately before his
departure from Abbotsford, for Naples.

Composed 1831.—Published 1835

THE gallant Youth, who may have gained,
  Or seeks, a ' winsome Marrow ',
Was but an Infant in the lap
  When first I looked on Yarrow ;
Once more, by Newark's Castle-gate   5
  Long left without a warder,
I stood, looked, listened, and with Thee,
  Great Minstrel of the Border !

Grave thoughts ruled wide on that sweet day,
  Their dignity installing   10
In gentle bosoms, while sere leaves
  Were on the bough, or falling ;
But breezes played, and sunshine gleamed—
  The forest to embolden ;
Reddened the fiery hues, and shot   15
  Transparence through the golden.

For busy thoughts the Stream flowed on
  In foamy agitation ;
And slept in many a crystal pool
  For quiet contemplation :   20
No public and no private care
  The freeborn mind enthralling,
We made a day of happy hours,
  Our happy days recalling.

Brisk Youth appeared, the Morn of Youth,   25
  With freaks of graceful folly,—
Life's temperate Noon, her sober Eve,
  Her Night not melancholy ;
Past, present, future, all appeared
  In harmony united,   30
Like guests that meet, and some from far,
  By cordial love invited.

And if, as Yarrow, through the woods
  And down the meadow ranging,
Did meet us with unaltered face,   35
  Though we were changed and changing ;
If, *then*, some natural shadows spread
  Our inward prospect over,
The soul's deep valley was not slow
  Its brightness to recover.   40

Eternal blessing on the Muse,
  And her divine employment !
The blameless Muse, who trains her sons
  For hope and calm enjoyment ;
Albeit sickness, lingering yet,   45
  Has o'er their pillow brooded ;
And Care waylays their steps—a Sprite
  Not easily eluded.

For thee, O Scott ! compelled to change
  Green Eildon-hill and Cheviot   50
For warm Vesuvio's vine-clad slopes ;
  And leave thy Tweed and Tiviot
For mild Sorento's breezy waves ;
  May classic Fancy, linking
With native Fancy her fresh aid,   55
  Preserve thy heart from sinking !

Oh! while they minister to thee,
  Each vying with the other,
May Health return to mellow Age,
  With Strength, her venturous brother; 60
And Tiber, and each brook and rill
  Renowned in song and story,
With unimagined beauty shine,
  Nor lose one ray of glory!

For Thou, upon a hundred streams, 65
  By tales of love and sorrow,
Of faithful love, undaunted truth,
  Hast shed the power of Yarrow;
And streams unknown, hills yet unseen,
  Wherever they invite Thee, 70
At parent Nature's grateful call,
  With gladness must requite Thee.

A gracious welcome shall be thine,
  Such looks of love and honour
As thy own Yarrow gave to me 75
  When first I gazed upon her;
Beheld what I had feared to see,
  Unwilling to surrender
Dreams treasured up from early days,
  The holy and the tender. 80

And what, for this frail world, were all
  That mortals do or suffer,
Did no responsive harp, no pen,
  Memorial tribute offer?
Yea, what were mighty Nature's self? 85
  Her features, could they win us,
Unhelped by the poetic voice
  That hourly speaks within us?

Nor deem that localised Romance
  Plays false with our affections ;   90
Unsanctifies our tears—made sport
  For fanciful dejections :
Ah, no ! the visions of the past
  Sustain the heart in feeling
Life as she is—our changeful Life,   95
  With friends and kindred dealing.

Bear witness, Ye, whose thoughts that day
  In Yarrow's groves were centred ;
Who through the silent portal arch
  Of mouldering Newark entered ;   100
And clomb the winding stair that once
  Too timidly was mounted
By the ' last Minstrel ', (not the last !)
  Ere he his Tale recounted.

Flow on for ever, Yarrow Stream !   105
  Fulfil thy pensive duty,
Well pleased that future Bards should chant
  For simple hearts thy beauty ;
To dream-light dear while yet unseen,
  Dear to the common sunshine,   110
And dearer still, as now I feel,
  To memory's shadowy moonshine !

EXTEMPORE EFFUSION

UPON THE

DEATH OF JAMES HOGG

Composed November 1835.—Published December 12, 1835 (*The Athenæum*) ; ed. 1837

WHEN first, descending from the moorlands,
I saw the Stream of Yarrow glide
Along a bare and open valley,
The Ettrick Shepherd was my guide.

When last along its banks I wandered,   5
Through groves that had begun to shed
Their golden leaves upon the pathways,
My steps the Border-minstrel led.

The mighty Minstrel breathes no longer,
'Mid mouldering ruins low he lies ;   10
And death upon the braes of Yarrow,
Has closed the Shepherd-poet's eyes :

Nor has the rolling year twice measured,
From sign to sign, its steadfast course,
Since every mortal power of Coleridge   15
Was frozen at its marvellous source ;

The rapt One, of the godlike forehead,
The heaven-eyed creature sleeps in earth :
And Lamb, the frolic and the gentle,
Has vanished from his lonely hearth.   20

Like clouds that rake the mountain-summits,
Or waves that own no curbing hand,
How fast has brother followed brother,
From sunshine to the sunless land !

Yet I, whose lids from infant slumber   25
Were earlier raised, remain to hear
A timid voice, that asks in whispers,
' Who next will drop and disappear ? '

Our haughty life is crowned with darkness,
Like London with its own black wreath,   30
On which with thee, O Crabbe ! forth-looking,
I gazed on Hampstead's breezy heath.

As if but yesterday departed,
Thou too art gone before ; but why,
O'er ripe fruit, seasonably gathered,   35
Should frail survivors heave a sigh ?

Mourn rather for that holy Spirit,
Sweet as the spring, as ocean deep ;
For Her who, ere her summer faded,
Has sunk into a breathless sleep.   40

No more of old romantic sorrows,
For slaughtered Youth or love-lorn Maid !
With sharper grief is Yarrow smitten,
And Ettrick mourns with her their Poet dead.

SONNETS

Composed ?.—Published 1807

NUNS fret not at their convent's narrow room ;
And hermits are contented with their cells ;
And students with their pensive citadels ;
Maids at the wheel, the weaver at his loom,
Sit blithe and happy ; bees that soar for bloom,   5
High as the highest Peak of Furness-fells,
Will murmur by the hour in foxglove bells :
In truth the prison, unto which we doom
Ourselves, no prison is : and hence for me,
In sundry moods, 'twas pastime to be bound   10
Within the Sonnet's scanty plot of ground ;
Pleased if some Souls (for such there needs must be)
Who have felt the weight of too much liberty,
Should find brief solace there, as I have found.

Composed ?.—Published 1827

SCORN not the Sonnet ; Critic, you have frowned,
Mindless of its just honours ; with this key
Shakspeare unlocked his heart ; the melody
Of this small lute gave ease to Petrarch's wound ;
A thousand times this pipe did Tasso sound ;   5
With it Camöens soothed an exile's grief ;
The Sonnet glittered a gay myrtle leaf
Amid the cypress with which Dante crowned
His visionary brow : a glow-worm lamp,
It cheered mild Spenser, called from Faery-land   10
To struggle through dark ways ; and when a damp
Fell round the path of Milton, in his hand
The Thing became a trumpet ; whence he blew
Soul-animating strains—alas, too few !

1801

Composed May 21, 1802.—Published September 6, 1802 (*Morning Post*); January 29, 1803 (*Ibid.*); 1807

I GRIEVED for Buonaparté, with a vain
And an unthinking grief! The tenderest mood
Of that Man's mind—what can it be? what food
Fed his first hopes? what knowledge could *he* gain?
'Tis not in battles that from youth we train   5
The Governor who must be wise and good,
And temper with the sternness of the brain
Thoughts motherly, and meek as womanhood.
Wisdom doth live with children round her knees:
Books, leisure, perfect freedom, and the talk   10
Man holds with week-day man in the hourly walk
Of the mind's business: these are the degrees
By which true Sway doth mount; this is the stalk
True Power doth grow on; and her rights are these.

COMPOSED UPON WESTMINSTER BRIDGE

SEPTEMBER 3, 1802

Composed July 31, 1802.—Published 1807

EARTH has not anything to show more fair:
Dull would he be of soul who could pass by
A sight so touching in its majesty:
This City now doth, like a garment, wear
The beauty of the morning; silent, bare,   5
Ships, towers, domes, theatres, and temples lie
Open unto the fields, and to the sky;
All bright and glittering in the smokeless air.
Never did sun more beautifully steep   C
In his first splendour, valley, rock, or hill;   ◌   10
Ne'er saw I, never felt, a calm so deep!   ◌
The river glideth at his own sweet will: ◌
Dear God! the very houses seem asleep;   ◌
And all that mighty heart is lying still!   ◌

Composed August, 1802.—Published 1807

IT is a beauteous evening, calm and free,
The holy time is quiet as a Nun
Breathless with adoration ; the broad sun
Is sinking down in its tranquillity ;
The gentleness of heaven broods o'er the Sea : 5
Listen ! the mighty Being is awake,
And doth with his eternal motion make
A sound like thunder—everlastingly.
Dear Child ! dear Girl ! that walkest with me here,
If thou appear untouched by solemn thought, 10
Thy nature is not therefore less divine :
Thou liest in Abraham's bosom all the year ;
And worshipp'st at the Temple's inner shrine,
God being with thee when we know it not.

ON THE EXTINCTION OF THE
VENETIAN REPUBLIC

Composed probably August 1802.—Published 1807

ONCE did She hold the gorgeous east in fee ;
And was the safeguard of the west : the worth
Of Venice did not fall below her birth,
Venice, the eldest Child of Liberty.
She was a maiden City, bright and free ; 5
No guile seduced, no force could violate ;
And, when she took unto herself a Mate,
She must espouse the everlasting Sea.
And what if she had seen those glories fade,
Those titles vanish, and that strength decay ; 10
Yet shall some tribute of regret be paid
When her long life hath reached its final day :
Men are we, and must grieve when even the Shade
Of that which once was great is passed away.

TO TOUSSAINT L'OUVERTURE

Composed probably August 1802.—Published February **2,** 1803
(*Morning Post*) ; 1807

TOUSSAINT, the most unhappy man of men !
Whether the whistling Rustic tend his plough
Within thy hearing, or thy head be now
Pillowed in some deep dungeon's earless den ;—
O miserable Chieftain ! where and when   5
Wilt thou find patience ! Yet die not ; do thou
Wear rather in thy bonds a cheerful brow :
Though fallen thyself, never to rise again,
Live, and take comfort. Thou hast left behind
Powers that will work for thee ; air, earth, and skies; 10
There 's not a breathing of the common wind
That will forget thee ; thou hast great allies ;
Thy friends are exultations, agonies,
And love, and man's unconquerable mind.

SEPTEMBER, 1802. NEAR DOVER

Composed September 1802.—Published 1807

INLAND, within a hollow vale, I stood ;
And saw, while sea was calm and air was clear,
The coast of France—the coast of France how near !
Drawn almost into frightful neighbourhood.
I shrunk ; for verily the barrier flood   5
Was like a lake, or river bright and fair,
A span of waters ; yet what power is there !
What mightiness for evil and for good !
Even so doth God protect us if we be
Virtuous and wise. Winds blow, and waters roll,   10
Strength to the brave, and Power, and Deity ;
Yet in themselves are nothing ! One decree
Spake laws to *them*, and said that by the soul
Only, the Nations shall be great and free.

WRITTEN IN LONDON, SEPTEMBER, 1802

Composed September 1802.—Published 1807

O FRIEND ! I know not which way I must look
For comfort, being, as I am, opprest,
To think that now our life is only drest
For show ; mean handy-work of craftsman, cook,
Or groom !—We must run glittering like a brook   5
In the open sunshine, or we are unblest :
The wealthiest man among us is the best :
No grandeur now in nature or in book
Delights us.   Rapine, avarice, expense,
This is idolatry ; and these we adore :   10
Plain living and high thinking are no more :
The homely beauty of the good old cause
Is gone ; our peace, our fearful innocence,
And pure religion breathing household laws.

LONDON, 1802

Composed September 1802.—Published 1807

MILTON ! thou shouldst be living at this hour :
England hath need of thee : she is a fen
Of stagnant waters : altar, sword, and pen,
Fireside, the heroic wealth of hall and bower,
Have forfeited their ancient English dower   5
Of inward happiness.   We are selfish men ;
Oh ! raise us up, return to us again ;
And give us manners, virtue, freedom, power.
Thy soul was like a Star, and dwelt apart ;
Thou hadst a voice whose sound was like the sea :   10
Pure as the naked heavens, majestic, free,
So didst thou travel on life's common way,
In cheerful godliness ; and yet thy heart
The lowliest duties on herself did lay.

Composed 1802 or 1803.—Published April 16, 1803 (*Morning Post*); 1807

IT is not to be thought of that the Flood
Of British freedom, which, to the open sea
Of the world's praise, from dark antiquity
Hath flowed, ' with pomp of waters, unwithstood,'
Roused though it be full often to a mood   5
Which spurns the check of salutary bands,
That this most famous Stream in bogs and sands
Should perish ; and to evil and to good
Be lost for ever.   In our halls is hung
Armoury of the invincible Knights of old :   10
We must be free or die, who speak the tongue
That Shakspeare spake ; the faith and morals hold
Which Milton held.—In every thing we are sprung
Of Earth's first blood, have titles manifold.

Composed 1802 or 1803.—Published September 17, 1803 (*Morning Post*) ; 1807

WHEN I have borne in memory what has tamed
Great Nations, how ennobling thoughts depart
When men change swords for ledgers, and desert
The student's bower for gold, some fears unnamed
I had, my Country—am I to be blamed ?   5
Now, when I think of thee, and what thou art,
Verily, in the bottom of my heart,
Of those unfilial fears I am ashamed.
For dearly must we prize thee ; we who find
In thee a bulwark for the cause of men ;   10
And I by my affection was beguiled :
What wonder if a Poet now and then,
Among the many movements of his mind,
Felt for thee as a lover or a child !

NOVEMBER, 1806

Composed 1806.—Published 1807

ANOTHER year !—another deadly blow !
Another mighty Empire overthrown !
And We are left, or shall be left, alone ;
The last that dare to struggle with the Foe.
'Tis well ! from this day forward we shall know   5
That in ourselves our safety must be sought ;
That by our own right hands it must be wrought ;
That we must stand unpropped, or be laid low.
O dastard whom such foretaste doth not cheer !
We shall exult, if they who rule the land   10
Be men who hold its many blessings dear,
Wise, upright, valiant ; not a servile band,
Who are to judge of danger which they fear,
And honour which they do not understand.

THOUGHT OF A BRITON ON THE
SUBJUGATION OF SWITZERLAND

Composed probably early in 1807.—Published 1807

Two Voices are there ; one is of the sea,
One of the mountains ; each a mighty Voice :
In both from age to age thou didst rejoice,
They were thy chosen music, Liberty !
There came a Tyrant, and with holy glee   5
Thou fought'st against him ; but hast vainly striven :
Thou from thy Alpine holds at length art driven,
Where not a torrent murmurs heard by thee.
Of one deep bliss thine ear hath been bereft :
Then cleave, O cleave to that which still is left ;   10
For, high-souled Maid, what sorrow would it be
That Mountain floods should thunder as before,
And Ocean bellow from his rocky shore,
And neither awful Voice be heard by thee !

3 Sins

The world - The flesh - The devil

146

Composed ?.—Published 1807

General
1)
2)
3)

separati

advantage

THE world is too much with us; late and soon,
Getting and spending, we lay waste our powers:
Little we see in Nature that is ours;
We have given our hearts away, a sordid boon!
This Sea that <u>bares her bosom</u> to the moon;
The winds that will be <u>howling</u> at all hours,
And are up-gathered now like <u>sleeping</u> flowers;
For this, for everything, we are out of tune;
It moves us not.—Great God! I'd rather be
A Pagan <u>suckled</u> in a <u>creed outworn</u>;
So might I, standing on this pleasant lea,
Have glimpses that would make me less forlorn;
Have sight of Proteus rising from the sea;
Or hear old Triton blow his wreathèd horn.

junction

5

10

(Stop & smell the roses)

If you get this one wrong, the rest goes wrong.

COMPOSED WHILE THE AUTHOR WAS ENGAGED IN
WRITING A TRACT OCCASIONED BY

THE CONVENTION OF CINTRA

Composed November or December 1808.—Published 1815

NOT 'mid the World's vain objects that enslave
The free-born Soul—that World whose vaunted skill
In selfish interest perverts the will,
Whose factions lead astray the wise and brave—
Not there; but in dark wood and rocky cave,
And hollow vale which foaming torrents fill
With omnipresent murmur as they rave
Down their steep beds, that never shall be still:
Here, mighty Nature! in this school sublime
I weigh the hopes and fears of suffering Spain;
For her consult the auguries of time,
And through the human heart explore my way;
And look and listen—gathering, whence I may,
Triumph, and thoughts no bondage can restrain.

5

10

1811

Composed 1811.—Published 1815

HERE pause : the poet claims at least this praise,
That virtuous Liberty hath been the scope
Of his pure song, which did not shrink from hope
In the worst moment of these evil days ;
From hope, the paramount *duty* that Heaven lays,   5
For its own honour, on man's suffering heart.
Never may from our souls one truth depart—
That an accursed thing it is to gaze
On prosperous tyrants with a dazzled eye ;
Nor—touched with due abhorrence of *their* guilt   10
For whose dire ends tears flow, and blood is spilt,
And justice labours in extremity—
Forget thy weakness, upon which is built,
O wretched man, the throne of tyranny !

UPON THE SIGHT OF A BEAUTIFUL PICTURE

Composed August 1811.—Published 1815

PRAISED be the Art whose subtle power could stay
Yon cloud, and fix it in that glorious shape ;
Nor would permit the thin smoke to escape,
Nor those bright sunbeams to forsake the day ;
Which stopped that band of travellers on their way,   5
Ere they were lost within the shady wood ;
And showed the Bark upon the glassy flood
For ever anchored in her sheltering bay.
Soul-soothing Art ! whom Morning, Noontide, Even,
Do serve with all their changeful pageantry ;   10
Thou, with ambition modest yet sublime,
Here, for the sight of mortal man, hast given
To one brief moment caught from fleeting time
The appropriate calm of blest eternity.

Composed ?.—Published 1815

HAIL, Twilight, sovereign of one peaceful hour !
Not dull art Thou as undiscerning Night ;
But studious only to remove from sight
Day's mutable distinctions.—Ancient Power !
Thus did the waters gleam, the mountains lower,   5
To the rude Briton, when, in wolf-skin vest
Here roving wild, he laid him down to rest
On the bare rock, or through a leafy bower
Looked ere his eyes were closed. By him was seen
The self-same Vision which we now behold,   10
At thy meek bidding, shadowy Power ! brought forth ;
These mighty barriers, and the gulf between ;
The flood, the stars,—a spectacle as old
As the beginning of the heavens and earth !

AFTER-THOUGHT

Composed ?.—Published 1820

I thought of Thee, my partner and my guide,
As being past away.—Vain sympathies !
For, backward, Duddon ! as I cast my eyes,
I see what was, and is, and will abide ;
Still glides the Stream, and shall for ever glide ;   5
The Form remains, the Function never dies ;
While we, the brave, the mighty, and the wise,
We Men, who in our morn of youth defied
The elements, must vanish ;—be it so !
Enough, if something from our hands have power   10
To live, and act, and serve the future hour ;
And if, as toward the silent tomb we go,
Through love, through hope, and faith's transcendent dower,
We feel that we are greater than we know.

ON THE DEPARTURE OF

SIR WALTER SCOTT

FROM ABBOTSFORD, FOR NAPLES

Composed September 1831.—Published 1833 (*Literary Souvenir* of
Alaric Watts) ; vol. of 1835

A TROUBLE, not of clouds, or weeping rain,
Nor of the setting sun's pathetic light
Engendered, hangs o'er Eildon's triple height :
Spirits of Power, assembled there, complain
For kindred Power departing from their sight ;   5
While Tweed, best pleased in chanting a blithe strain,
Saddens his voice again, and yet again.
Lift up your hearts, ye Mourners ! for the might
Of the whole world's good wishes with him goes :
Blessings and prayers in nobler retinue   10
Than sceptred king or laurelled conquerer knows,
Follow this wondrous Potentate. Be true,
Ye winds of ocean, and the midland sea,
Wafting your Charge to soft Parthenope !

Composed 1833.—Published 1835

MOST sweet it is with unuplifted eyes
To pace the ground, if path be there or none,
While a fair region round the traveller lies
Which he forbears again to look upon :
Pleased rather with some soft ideal scene,   5
The work of Fancy, or some happy tone
Of meditation, slipping in between
The beauty coming and the beauty gone.
If Thought and Love desert us, from that day
Let us break off all commerce with the Muse :   10
With Thought and Love companions of our way,
Whate'er the senses take or may refuse,
The Mind's internal heaven shall shed her dews
Of inspiration on the humblest lay.

PREFACE TO
LYRICAL BALLADS

THE first volume of these Poems has already been submitted to general perusal. It was published, as an experiment, which, I hoped, might be of some use to ascertain, how far, by fitting to metrical arrangement a selection of the real language of men in a state of vivid sensation, that sort of pleasure and that quantity of pleasure may be imparted, which a Poet may rationally endeavour to impart.

I had formed no very inaccurate estimate of the probable effect of those Poems : I flattered myself that they who
10 should be pleased with them would read them with more than common pleasure : and, on the other hand, I was well aware, that by those who should dislike them they would be read with more than common dislike. The result has differed from my expectation in this only, that a greater number have been pleased than I ventured to hope I should please.

. . . .

Several of my Friends are anxious for the success of these Poems, from a belief, that, if the views with which they were composed were indeed realized, a class of Poetry would be
20 produced, well adapted to interest mankind permanently, and not unimportant in the quality, and in the multiplicity of its moral relations : and on this account they have advised me to prefix a systematic defence of the theory upon which the Poems were written. But I was unwilling to undertake the task, knowing that on this occasion the Reader would look coldly upon my arguments, since I might be suspected of having been principally influenced by the selfish and foolish hope of *reasoning* him into an approbation of these particular Poems : and I was still more unwilling

to undertake the task, because adequately to display the
opinions, and fully to enforce the arguments, would require
a space wholly disproportionate to a preface. For, to treat
the subject with the clearness and coherence of which it is
susceptible, it would be necessary to give a full account of
the present state of the public taste in this country, and to
determine how far this taste is healthy or depraved ; which,
again, could not be determined, without pointing out in
what manner language and the human mind act and re-act
on each other, and without retracing the revolutions, not of 10
literature alone, but likewise of society itself. I have therefore altogether declined to enter regularly upon this defence ;
yet I am sensible, that there would be something like im-
propriety in abruptly obtruding upon the Public, without
a few words of introduction, Poems so materially different
from those upon which general approbation is at present
bestowed.

It is supposed, that by the act of writing in verse an Author
makes a formal engagement that he will gratify certain
known habits of association ; that he not only thus apprises 20
the Reader that certain classes of ideas and expressions will
be found in his book, but that others will be carefully excluded. This exponent or symbol held forth by metrical
language must in different eras of literature have excited
very different expectations : for example, in the age of
Catullus, Terence, and Lucretius, and that of Statius or
Claudian ; and in our own country, in the age of Shakespeare and Beaumont and Fletcher, and that of Donne and
Cowley, or Dryden, or Pope. I will not take upon me to
determine the exact import of the promise which, by the act 30
of writing in verse, an Author in the present day makes to
his Reader : but it will undoubtedly appear to many persons
that I have not fulfilled the terms of an engagement thus
voluntarily contracted. They who have been accustomed
to the gaudiness and inane phraseology of many modern

writers, if they persist in reading this book to its conclusion, will, no doubt, frequently have to struggle with feelings of strangeness and awkwardness : they will look round for poetry, and will be induced to inquire by what species of courtesy these attempts can be permitted to assume that title. I hope therefore the Reader will not censure me for attempting to state what I have proposed to myself to perform ; and also (as far as the limits of a preface will permit) to explain some of the chief reasons which have determined
10 me in the choice of my purpose : that at least he may be spared any unpleasant feeling of disappointment, and that I myself may be protected from one of the most dishonourable accusations which can be brought against an Author ; namely, that of an indolence which prevents him from endeavouring to ascertain what is his duty, or, when his duty is ascertained, prevents him from performing it.

The principal object, then, proposed in these Poems was to choose incidents and situations from common life, and to relate or describe them, throughout, as far as was possible
20 in a selection of language really used by men, and, at the same time, to throw over them a certain colouring of imagination, whereby ordinary things should be presented to the mind in an unusual aspect ; and, further, and above all, to make these incidents and situations interesting by tracing in them, truly though not ostentatiously, the primary laws of our nature : chiefly, as far as regards the manner in which we associate ideas in a state of excitement. Humble and rustic life was generally chosen, because, in that condition, the essential passions of the heart find a
30 better soil in which they can attain their maturity, are less under restraint, and speak a plainer and more emphatic language ; because in that condition of life our elementary feelings coexist in a state of greater simplicity, and, consequently, may be more accurately contemplated, and more forcibly communicated ; because the manners of rural life

germinate from those elementary feelings, and, from the necessary character of rural occupations, are more easily comprehended, and are more durable ; and, lastly, because in that condition the passions of men are incorporated with the beautiful and permanent forms of nature. The language, too, of these men has been adopted (purified indeed from what appear to be its real defects, from all lasting and rational causes of dislike or disgust) because such men hourly communicate with the best objects from which the best part of language is originally derived ; and because, from their rank in society and the sameness and narrow circle of their intercourse, being less under the influence of social vanity, they convey their feelings and notions in simple and unelaborated expressions. Accordingly, such a language, arising out of repeated experience and regular feelings, is a more permanent, and a far more philosophical language, than that which is frequently substituted for it by Poets, who think that they are conferring honour upon themselves and their art, in proportion as they separate themselves from the sympathies of men, and indulge in arbitrary and capricious habits of expression, in order to furnish food for fickle tastes, and fickle appetites, of their own creation.[1]

I cannot, however, be insensible to the present outcry against the triviality and meanness, both of thought and language, which some of my contemporaries have occasionally introduced into their metrical compositions ; and I acknowledge that this defect, where it exists, is more dishonourable to the Writer's own character than false refinement or arbitrary innovation, though I should contend at the same time, that it is far less pernicious in the sum of its consequences. From such verses the Poems in these volumes will be found distinguished at least by one mark

[1] It is worth while here to observe, that the affecting parts of Chaucer are almost always expressed in language pure and universally intelligible even to this day.

of difference, that each of them has a worthy *purpose*. Not that I always began to write with a distinct purpose formally conceived ; but habits of meditation have, I trust, so prompted and regulated my feelings, that my descriptions of such objects as strongly excite those feelings, will be found to carry along with them a *purpose*. If this opinion be erroneous, I can have little right to the name of a Poet. For all good poetry is the spontaneous overflow of powerful feelings : and though this be true, Poems to which any value
10 can be attached were never produced on any variety of subjects but by a man who, being possessed of more than usual organic sensibility, had also thought long and deeply. For our continued influxes of feeling are modified and directed by our thoughts, which are indeed the representatives of all our past feelings ; and, as by contemplating the relation of these general representatives to each other, we discover what is really important to men, so, by the repetition and continuance of this act, our feelings will be connected with important subjects, till at length, if we be
20 originally possessed of much sensibility, such habits of mind will be produced, that, by obeying blindly and mechanically the impulses of those habits, we shall describe objects, and utter sentiments, of such a nature, and in such connexion with each other, that the understanding of the Reader must necessarily be in some degree enlightened, and his affections strengthened and purified.

It has been said that each of these poems has a purpose. Another circumstance must be mentioned which distinguishes these Poems from the popular Poetry of the day ;
30 it is this, that the feeling therein developed gives importance to the action and situation, and not the action and situation to the feeling.

A sense of false modesty shall not prevent me from asserting, that the Reader's attention is pointed to this mark of distinction, far less for the sake of these particular Poems

than from the general importance of the subject. The
subject is indeed important ! For the human mind is
capable of being excited without the application of gross
and violent stimulants ; and he must have a very faint
perception of its beauty and dignity who does not know this,
and who does not further know, that one being is elevated
above another, in proportion as he possesses this capability.
It has therefore appeared to me, that to endeavour to produce or enlarge this capability is one of the best services in
which, at any period, a Writer can be engaged ; but this 10
service, excellent at all times, is especially so at the present
day. For a multitude of causes, unknown to former times,
are now acting with a combined force to blunt the dis-
criminating powers of the mind, and, unfitting it for all
voluntary exertion, to reduce it to a state of almost savage
torpor. The most effective of these causes are the great
national events which are daily taking place, and the increasing accumulation of men in cities, where the uniformity
of their occupations produces a craving for extraordinary
incident, which the rapid communication of intelligence 20
hourly gratifies. To this tendency of life and manners the
literature and theatrical exhibitions of the country have
conformed themselves. The invaluable works of our elder
writers, I had almost said the works of Shakespeare and
Milton, are driven into neglect by frantic novels, sickly and
stupid German Tragedies, and deluges of idle and extrava-
gant stories in verse.—When I think upon this degrading
thirst after outrageous stimulation, I am almost ashamed
to have spoken of the feeble endeavour made in these
volumes to counteract it ; and, reflecting upon the magni- 30
tude of the general evil, I should be oppressed with no
dishonourable melancholy, had I not a deep impression of
certain inherent and indestructible qualities of the human
mind, and likewise of certain powers in the great and permanent objects that act upon it, which are equally inherent

and indestructible ; and were there not added to this impression a belief, that the time is approaching when the evil
will be systematically opposed, by men of greater powers,
and with far more distinguished success.

Having dwelt thus long on the subjects and aim of these
Poems, I shall request the Reader's permission to apprise
him of a few circumstances relating to their *style*, in order,
among other reasons, that he may not censure me for not
having performed what I never attempted.   The Reader
10 will find that personifications of abstract ideas rarely occur
in these volumes ; and are utterly rejected, as an ordinary
device to elevate the style, and raise it above prose.   My
purpose was to imitate, and, as far as possible, to adopt the
very language of men ; and assuredly such personifications
do not make any natural or regular part of that language.
They are, indeed, a figure of speech occasionally prompted
by passion, and I have made use of them as such ; but have
endeavoured utterly to reject them as a mechanical device
of style, or as a family language which Writers in metre seem
20 to lay claim to by prescription.   I have wished to keep the
Reader in the company of flesh and blood, persuaded that
by so doing I shall interest him.   Others who pursue a
different track will interest him likewise ; I do not interfere
with their claim, but wish to prefer a claim of my own.   There
will also be found in these volumes little of what is usually
called poetic diction ; as much pains has been taken to
avoid it as is ordinarily taken to produce it ; this has been
done for the reason already alleged, to bring my language
near to the language of men ; and further, because the
30 pleasure which I have proposed to myself to impart, is of
a kind very different from that which is supposed by many
persons to be the proper object of poetry.   Without being
culpably particular, I do not know how to give my Reader
a more exact notion of the style in which it was my wish and
intention to write, than by informing him that I have at all

times endeavoured to look steadily at my subject ; consequently, there is I hope in these Poems little falsehood of
description, and my ideas are expressed in language fitted
to their respective importance. Something must have been
gained by this practice, as it is friendly to one property
of all good poetry, namely, good sense : but it has necessarily cut me off from a large portion of phrases and figures
of speech which from father to son have long been regarded
as the common inheritance of Poets. I have also thought
it expedient to restrict myself still further, having abstained 10
from the use of many expressions, in themselves proper and
beautiful, but which have been foolishly repeated by bad
Poets, till such feelings of disgust are connected with them
as it is scarcely possible by any art of association to over-
power.

If in a poem there should be found a series of lines, or
even a single line, in which the language, though naturally
arranged, and according to the strict laws of metre, does
not differ from that of prose, there is a numerous class of
critics, who, when they stumble upon these prosaisms, as 20
they call them, imagine that they have made a notable
discovery, and exult over the Poet as over a man ignorant
of his own profession. Now these men would establish
a canon of criticism which the Reader will conclude he must
utterly reject, if he wishes to be pleased with these volumes.
And it would be a most easy task to prove to him, that not
only the language of a large portion of every good poem,
even of the most elevated character, must necessarily,
except with reference to the metre, in no respect differ from
that of good prose, but likewise that some of the most inter- 30
esting parts of the best poems will be found to be strictly the
language of prose when prose is well written. The truth of
this assertion might be demonstrated by innumerable
passages from almost all the poetical writings, even of
Milton himself. To illustrate the subject in a general

manner, I will here adduce a short composition of Gray, who
was at the head of those who, by their reasonings, have
attempted to widen the space of separation betwixt Prose
and Metrical composition, and was more than any other
man curiously elaborate in the structure of his own poetic
diction.

> In vain to me the smiling mornings shine,
> And reddening Phoebus lifts his golden fire :
> The birds in vain their amorous descant join,
> Or cheerful fields resume their green attire.
> These ears, alas ! for other notes repine ;
> *A different object do these eyes require ;*
> *My lonely anguish melts no heart but mine ;*
> *And in my breast the imperfect joys expire ;*
> Yet morning smiles the busy race to cheer,
> And new-born pleasure brings to happier men ;
> The fields to all their wonted tribute bear ;
> To warm their little loves the birds complain,
> *I fruitless mourn to him that cannot hear,*
> *And weep the more because I weep in vain.*

It will easily be perceived, that the only part of this
Sonnet which is of any value is the lines printed in Italics ;
it is equally obvious, that, except in the rhyme, and in the
use of the single word ' fruitless ' for fruitlessly, which is so
far a defect, the language of these lines does in no respect
differ from that of prose.

By the foregoing quotation it has been shown that the language of Prose may yet be well adapted to Poetry ; and it
was previously asserted, that a large portion of the language
of every good poem can in no respect differ from that of
good Prose. We will go further. It may be safely affirmed,
that there neither is, nor can be, any *essential* difference
between the language of prose and metrical composition.
We are fond of tracing the resemblance between Poetry and
Painting, and, accordingly, we call them Sisters : but where
shall we find bonds of connexion sufficiently strict to typify

the affinity betwixt metrical and prose composition ? They both speak by and to the same organs ; the bodies in which both of them are clothed may be said to be of the same substance, their affections are kindred, and almost identical, not necessarily differing even in degree ; Poetry [1] sheds no tears ' such as Angels weep ', but natural and human tears ; she can boast of no celestial Ichor that distinguishes her vital juices from those of prose ; the same human blood circulates through the veins of them both.

If it be affirmed that rhyme and metrical arrangement [10] of themselves constitute a distinction which overturns what has just been said on the strict affinity of metrical language with that of prose, and paves the way for other artificial distinctions which the mind voluntarily admits, I answer that the language of such Poetry as is here recommended is, as far as is possible, a selection of the language really spoken by men ; that this selection, wherever it is made with true taste and feeling, will of itself form a distinction far greater than would at first be imagined, and will entirely separate the composition from the vulgarity and meanness of [20] ordinary life ; and, if metre be superadded thereto, I believe that a dissimilitude will be produced altogether sufficient for the gratification of a rational mind. What other distinction would we have ? Whence is it to come ? And where is it to exist ? Not, surely, where the Poet speaks through the mouths of his characters : it cannot be necessary here, either for elevation of style, or any of its supposed

[1] I here use the word ' Poetry ' (though against my own judgement) as opposed to the word Prose, and synonymous with metrical composition. But much confusion has been introduced into criticism by this contradistinction of Poetry and Prose, instead of the more philosophical one of Poetry and Matter of Fact, or Science. The only strict antithesis to Prose is Metre ; nor is this, in truth, a *strict* antithesis, because lines and passages of metre so naturally occur in writing prose, that it would be scarcely possible to avoid them, even were it desirable.

ornaments : for, if the Poet's subject be judiciously chosen, it will naturally, and upon fit occasion, lead him to passions the language of which, if selected truly and judiciously, must necessarily be dignified and variegated, and alive with metaphors and figures. I forbear to speak of an incongruity which would shock the intelligent Reader, should the Poet interweave any foreign splendour of his own with that which the passion naturally suggests : it is sufficient to say that such addition is unnecessary. And, surely, it is more
10 probable that those passages, which with propriety abound with metaphors and figures, will have their due effect, if, upon other occasions where the passions are of a milder character, the style also be subdued and temperate.

But, as the pleasure which I hope to give by the Poems now presented to the Reader must depend entirely on just notions upon this subject, and, as it is in itself of high importance to our taste and moral feelings, I cannot content myself with these detached remarks. And, if in what I am about to say, it shall appear to some that my labour is
20 unnecessary, and that I am like a man fighting a battle without enemies, such persons may be reminded, that, whatever be the language outwardly holden by men, a practical faith in the opinions which I am wishing to establish is almost unknown. If my conclusions are admitted, and carried as far as they must be carried if admitted at all, our judgements concerning the works of the greatest Poets both ancient and modern will be far different from what they are at present, both when we praise, and when we censure : and our moral feelings influencing and influenced
30 by these judgements will, I believe, be corrected and purified.

Taking up the subject, then, upon general grounds, let me ask, what is meant by the word Poet ? What is a Poet ? To whom does he address himself ? And what language is to be expected from him ?—He is a man speaking to men :

a man, it is true, endowed with more lively sensibility, more
enthusiasm and tenderness, who has a greater knowledge
of human nature, and a more comprehensive soul, than are
supposed to be common among mankind ; a man pleased
with his own passions and volitions, and who rejoices more
than other men in the spirit of life that is in him ; delighting
to contemplate similar volitions and passions as manifested
in the goings-on of the Universe, and habitually impelled
to create them where he does not find them. To these
qualities he has added a disposition to be affected more than 10
other men by absent things as if they were present ; an
ability of conjuring up in himself passions, which are indeed
far from being the same as those produced by real events,
yet (especially in those parts of the general sympathy which
are pleasing and delightful) do more nearly resemble the
passions produced by real events, than anything which, from
the motions of their own minds merely, other men are
accustomed to feel in themselves :—whence, and from
practice, he has acquired a greater readiness and power in
expressing what he thinks and feels, and especially those 20
thoughts and feelings which, by his own choice, or from the
structure of his own mind, arise in him without immediate
external excitement.

But whatever portion of this faculty we may suppose
even the greatest Poet to possess, there cannot be a doubt
that the language which it will suggest to him, must often,
in liveliness and truth, fall short of that which is uttered by
men in real life, under the actual pressure of those passions,
certain shadows of which the Poet thus produces, or feels to
be produced, in himself.   30

However exalted a notion we would wish to cherish of the
character of a Poet, it is obvious, that while he describes
and imitates passions, his employment is in some degree
mechanical, compared with the freedom and power of real
and substantial action and suffering. So that it will be the

wish of the Poet to bring his feelings near to those of the persons whose feelings he describes, nay, for short spaces of time, perhaps, to let himself slip into an entire delusion, and even confound and identify his own feelings with theirs ; modifying only the language which is thus suggested to him by a consideration that he describes for a particular purpose, that of giving pleasure.   Here, then, he will apply the principle of selection which has been already insisted upon.   He will depend upon this for removing what would otherwise
10 be painful or disgusting in the passion ; he will feel that there is no necessity to trick out or to elevate nature : and, the more industriously he applies this principle, the deeper will be his faith that no words, which *his* fancy or imagination can suggest, will be to be compared with those which are the emanations of reality and truth.

But it may be said by those who do not object to the general spirit of these remarks, that, as it is impossible for the Poet to produce upon all occasions language as exquisitely fitted for the passion as that which the real passion
20 itself suggests, it is proper that he should consider himself as in the situation of a translator, who does not scruple to substitute excellencies of another kind for those which are unattainable by him ; and endeavours occasionally to surpass his original, in order to make some amends for the general inferiority to which he feels that he must submit. But this would be to encourage idleness and unmanly despair.   Further, it is the language of men who speak of what they do not understand ; who talk of Poetry as of a matter of amusement and idle pleasure ; who will converse with
30 us as gravely about a *taste* for Poetry, as they express it, as if it were a thing as indifferent as a taste for rope-dancing, or Frontiniac or Sherry.   Aristotle, I have been told, has said, that Poetry is the most philosophic of all writing : it is so : its object is truth, not individual and local, but general, and operative ; not standing upon external testimony, but

carried alive into the heart by passion ; truth which is its own testimony, which gives competence and confidence to the tribunal to which it appeals, and receives them from the same tribunal.   Poetry is the image of man and nature. The obstacles which stand in the way of the fidelity of the Biographer and Historian, and of their consequent utility, are incalculably greater than those which are to be encountered by the Poet who comprehends the dignity of his art.   The Poet writes under one restriction only, namely, the necessity of giving immediate pleasure to a human Being 10 possessed of that information which may be expected from him, not as a lawyer, a physician, a mariner, an astronomer, or a natural philosopher, but as a Man.   Except this one restriction, there is no object standing between the Poet and the image of things ; between this, and the Biographer and Historian, there are a thousand.

Nor let this necessity of producing immediate pleasure be considered as a degradation of the Poet's art.   It is far otherwise.   It is an acknowledgement of the beauty of the universe, an acknowledgement the more sincere, because 20 not formal, but indirect ; it is a task light and easy to him who looks at the world in the spirit of love : further, it is a homage paid to the native and naked dignity of man, to the grand elementary principle of pleasure, by which he knows and feels, and lives, and moves.   We have no sympathy but what is propagated by pleasure : I would not be misunderstood ; but wherever we sympathize with pain, it will be found that the sympathy is produced and carried on by subtle combinations with pleasure.   We have no knowledge, that is, no general principles drawn from the contem- 30 plation of particular facts, but what has been built up by pleasure, and exists in us by pleasure alone.   The Man of science, the Chemist and Mathematician, whatever difficulties and disgusts they may have had to struggle with, know and feel this.   However painful may be the objects

with which the Anatomist's knowledge is connected, he feels
that his knowledge is pleasure ; and where he has no pleasure he has no knowledge. What then does the Poet ? He
considers man and the objects that surround him as acting
and re-acting upon each other, so as to produce an infinite
complexity of pain and pleasure ; he considers man in his
own nature and in his ordinary life, as contemplating this
with a certain quantity of immediate knowledge, with
certain convictions, intuitions, and deductions, which from
10 habit acquire the quality of intuitions ; he considers him as
looking upon this complex scene of ideas and sensations, and
finding everywhere objects that immediately excite in him
sympathies which, from the necessities of his nature, are
accompanied by an overbalance of enjoyment.

To this knowledge which all men carry about with them,
and to these sympathies in which, without any other
discipline than that of our daily life, we are fitted to take
delight, the Poet principally directs his attention. He considers man and nature as essentially adapted to each other,
20 and the mind of man as naturally the mirror of the fairest
and most interesting properties of nature. And thus the
Poet, prompted by this feeling of pleasure, which accom-
panies him through the whole course of his studies, converses
with general nature, with affections akin to those, which,
through labour and length of time, the Man of science has
raised up in himself, by conversing with those particular
parts of nature which are the objects of his studies. The
knowledge both of the Poet and the Man of science is
pleasure ; but the knowledge of the one cleaves to us as
30 a necessary part of our existence, our natural and unalien-
able inheritance ; the other is a personal and individual
acquisition, slow to come to us, and by no habitual and
direct sympathy connecting us with our fellow-beings. The
Man of science seeks truth as a remote and unknown bene-
factor ; he cherishes and loves it in his solitude : the Poet,

singing a song in which all human beings join with him, rejoices in the presence of truth as our visible friend and hourly companion. Poetry is the breath and finer spirit of all knowledge ; it is the impassioned expression which is in the countenance of all Science. Emphatically may it be said of the Poet, as Shakespeare hath said of man, ' that he looks before and after.' He is the rock of defence for human nature ; an upholder and preserver, carrying everywhere with him relationship and love. In spite of difference of soil and climate, of language and manners, of laws and customs : 10 in spite of things silently gone out of mind, and things violently destroyed ; the Poet binds together by passion and knowledge the vast empire of human society, as it is spread over the whole earth, and over all time. The objects of the Poet's thoughts are everywhere ; though the eyes and senses of man are, it is true, his favourite guides, yet he will follow wheresoever he can find an atmosphere of sensation in which to move his wings. Poetry is the first and last of all knowledge—it is as immortal as the heart of man. If the labours of Men of science should ever create any material 20 revolution, direct or indirect, in our condition, and in the impressions which we habitually receive, the Poet will sleep then no more than at present ; he will be ready to follow the steps of the Man of science, not only in those general indirect effects, but he will be at his side, carrying sensation into the midst of the objects of the science itself. The remotest discoveries of the Chemist, the Botanist, or Mineralogist, will be as proper objects of the Poet's art as any upon which it can be employed, if the time should ever come when these things shall be familiar to us, and the relations under which 30 they are contemplated by the followers of these respective sciences shall be manifestly and palpably material to us as enjoying and suffering beings. If the time should ever come when what is now called science, thus familiarized to men, shall be ready to put on, as it were, a form of flesh and blood, the Poet will lend his divine spirit to aid the transfiguration, and will welcome the Being thus produced, as a dear and genuine inmate of the household of man.—It is not, then, to be supposed that any one, who holds that sublime notion of Poetry which I have attempted to convey, will break in upon the sanctity and truth of his pictures by transitory and accidental ornaments, and endeavour to excite admiration of himself by arts, the necessity of which must manifestly depend upon the assumed meanness of his subject.

10   What has been thus far said applies to Poetry in general ; but especially to those parts of composition where the Poet speaks through the mouths of his characters ; and upon this point it appears to authorize the conclusion that there are few persons of good sense, who would not allow that the dramatic parts of composition are defective, in proportion as they deviate from the real language of nature, and are coloured by a diction of the Poet's own, either peculiar to him as an individual Poet or belonging simply to Poets in general ; to a body of men who, from the circumstance of 20 their compositions being in metre, it is expected will employ a particular language.

It is not, then, in the dramatic parts of composition that we look for this distinction of language ; but still it may be proper and necessary where the Poet speaks to us in his own person and character. To this I answer by referring the Reader to the description before given of a Poet. Among the qualities there enumerated as principally conducing to form a Poet, is implied nothing differing in kind from other men, but only in degree. The sum of what was said is, that 30 the Poet is chiefly distinguished from other men by a greater promptness to think and feel without immediate external excitement, and a greater power in expressing such thoughts and feelings as are produced in him in that manner. But these passions and thoughts and feelings are the general passions and thoughts and feelings of men. And with what

are they connected ? Undoubtedly with our moral sentiments and animal sensations, and with the causes which
excite these ; with the operations of the elements, and the
appearances of the visible universe ; with storm and sunshine, with the revolutions of the seasons, with cold and
heat, with loss of friends and kindred, with injuries and
resentments, gratitude and hope, with fear and sorrow.
These, and the like, are the sensations and objects which the
Poet describes, as they are the sensations of other men, and
the objects which interest them. The Poet thinks and feels 10
in the spirit of human passions. How, then, can his language differ in any material degree from that of all other
men who feel vividly and see clearly ? It might be *proved*
that it is impossible. But supposing that this were not the
case, the Poet might then be allowed to use a peculiar language when expressing his feelings for his own gratification,
or that of men like himself. But Poets do not write for
Poets alone, but for men. Unless therefore we are advocates
for that admiration which subsists upon ignorance, and
that pleasure which arises from hearing what we do not 20
understand, the Poet must descend from this supposed
height ; and, in order to excite rational sympathy, he must
express himself as other men express themselves. To this
it may be added, that while he is only selecting from the
real language of men, or, which amounts to the same thing,
composing accurately in the spirit of such selection, he is
treading upon safe ground, and we know what we are to
expect from him. Our feelings are the same with respect to
metre ; for, as it may be proper to remind the Reader, the
distinction of metre is regular and uniform, and not, like that 30
which is produced by what is usually called POETIC DICTION,
arbitrary, and subject to infinite caprices upon which no
calculation whatever can be made. In the one case, the
Reader is utterly at the mercy of the Poet, respecting what
imagery or diction he may choose to connect with the

passion ; whereas, in the other, the metre obeys certain laws, to which the Poet and Reader both willingly submit because they are certain, and because no interference is made by them with the passion, but such as the concurring testimony of ages has shown to heighten and improve the pleasure which co-exists with it.

It will now be proper to answer an obvious question, namely, Why, professing these opinions, have I written in verse ? To this, in addition to such answer as is included in what has been already said, I reply, in the first place, Because, however I may have restricted myself, there is still left open to me what confessedly constitutes the most valuable object of all writing, whether in prose or verse ; the great and universal passions of men, the most general and interesting of their occupations, and the entire world of nature before me—to supply endless combinations of forms and imagery. Now, supposing for a moment that whatever is interesting in these objects may be as vividly described in prose, why should I be condemned for attempting to super-add to such description the charm which, by the consent of all nations, is acknowledged to exist in metrical language ? To this, by such as are yet unconvinced, it may be answered that a very small part of the pleasure given by Poetry depends upon the metre, and that it is injudicious to write in metre, unless it be accompanied with the other artificial distinctions of style with which metre is usually accompanied, and that, by such deviation, more will be lost from the shock which will thereby be given to the Reader's associations than will be counterbalanced by any pleasure which he can derive from the general power of numbers. In answer to those who still contend for the necessity of accompanying metre with certain appropriate colours of style in order to the accomplishment of its appropriate end, and who also, in my opinion, greatly underrate the power of metre in itself, it might, perhaps, as far as relates to these

Volumes, have been almost sufficient to observe, that poems
are extant, written upon more humble subjects, and in a still
more naked and simple style, which have continued to give
pleasure from generation to generation. Now, if nakedness
and simplicity be a defect, the fact here mentioned affords
a strong presumption that poems somewhat less naked and
simple are capable of affording pleasure at the present day ;
and, what I wished *chiefly* to attempt, at present, was to
justify myself for having written under the impression of
this belief.   10

But various causes might be pointed out why, when the
style is manly, and the subject of some importance, words
metrically arranged will long continue to impart such
a pleasure to mankind as he who proves the extent of that
pleasure will be desirous to impart. The end of Poetry is
to produce excitement in co-existence with an overbalance
of pleasure ; but, by the supposition, excitement is an
unusual and irregular state of the mind ; ideas and feelings
do not, in that state, succeed each other in accustomed
order. If the words, however, by which this excitement 20
is produced be in themselves powerful, or the images and
feelings have an undue proportion of pain connected with
them, there is some danger that the excitement may be
carried beyond its proper bounds. Now the co-presence of
something regular, something to which the mind has been
accustomed in various moods and in a less excited state,
cannot but have great efficacy in tempering and restraining
the passion by an intertexture of ordinary feeling, and of
feeling not strictly and necessarily connected with the
passion. This is unquestionably true ; and hence, though 30
the opinion will at first appear paradoxical, from the tendency of metre to divest language, in a certain degree, of its
reality, and thus to throw a sort of half-consciousness of
unsubstantial existence over the whole composition, there
can be little doubt but that more pathetic situations and

sentiments, that is, those which have a greater proportion of pain connected with them, may be endured in metrical composition, especially in rhyme, than in prose. The metre of the old ballads is very artless ; yet they contain many passages which would illustrate this opinion ; and, I hope, if the following Poems be attentively perused, similar instances will be found in them. This opinion may be further illustrated by appealing to the Reader's own experience of the reluctance with which he comes to the re-
10 perusal of the distressful parts of *Clarissa Harlowe*, or *The Gamester* ; while Shakespeare's writings, in the most pathetic scenes, never act upon us, as pathetic, beyond the bounds of pleasure—an effect which, in a much greater degree than might at first be imagined, is to be ascribed to small, but continual and regular impulses of pleasurable surprise from the metrical arrangement.—On the other hand (what it must be allowed will much more frequently happen) if the Poet's words should be incommensurate with the passion, and inadequate to raise the Reader to
20 a height of desirable excitement, then (unless the Poet's choice of his metre has been grossly injudicious), in the feelings of pleasure which the Reader has been accustomed to connect with metre in general, and in the feeling, whether cheerful or melancholy, which he has been accustomed to connect with that particular movement of metre, there will be found something which will greatly contribute to impart passion to the words, and to effect the complex end which the Poet proposes to himself.

If I had undertaken a SYSTEMATIC defence of the theory
30 here maintained, it would have been my duty to develop the various causes upon which the pleasure received from metrical language depends. Among the chief of these causes is to be reckoned a principle which must be well known to those who have made any of the Arts the object of accurate reflection ; namely, the pleasure which the mind derives

from the perception of similitude in dissimilitude.   This
principle is the great spring of the activity of our minds, and
their chief feeder.   From this principle the direction of the
sexual appetite, and all the passions connected with it, take
their origin : it is the life of our ordinary conversation ;
and upon the accuracy with which similitude in dissimilitude
and dissimilitude in similitude are perceived, depend our
taste and our moral feelings.   It would not be a useless
employment to apply this principle to the consideration of
metre, and to show that metre is hence enabled to afford 10
much pleasure, and to point out in what manner that
pleasure is produced.   But my limits will not permit me to
enter upon this subject, and I must content myself with
a general summary.

I have said that poetry is the spontaneous overflow of
powerful feelings : it takes its origin from emotion recollected in tranquillity : the emotion is contemplated till, by
a species of reaction, the tranquillity gradually disappears,
and an emotion, kindred to that which was before the subject of contemplation, is gradually produced, and does itself 20
actually exist in the mind.   In this mood successful composition generally begins, and in a mood similar to this it is
carried on ; but the emotion, of whatever kind, and in
whatever degree, from various causes, is qualified by various
pleasures, so that in describing any passions whatsoever,
which are voluntarily described, the mind will, upon the
whole, be in a state of enjoyment.   If Nature be thus
cautious to preserve in a state of enjoyment a being so
employed, the Poet ought to profit by the lesson held forth
to him, and ought especially to take care, that, whatever 30
passions he communicates to his Reader, those passions,
if his Reader's mind be sound and vigorous, should always
be accompanied with an overbalance of pleasure.   Now the
music of harmonious metrical language, the sense of difficulty overcome, and the blind association of pleasure which

has been previously received from works of rhyme or metre of the same or similar construction, an indistinct perception perpetually renewed of language closely resembling that of real life, and yet, in the circumstance of metre, differing from it so widely—all these imperceptibly make up a complex feeling of delight, which is of the most important use in tempering the painful feeling always found intermingled with powerful descriptions of the deeper passions. This effect is always produced in pathetic and impassioned poetry; while, in lighter compositions, the ease and gracefulness with which the Poet manages his numbers are themselves confessedly a principal source of the gratification of the Reader. All that it is *necessary* to say, however, upon this subject, may be effected by affirming, what few persons will deny, that, of two descriptions, either of passions, manners, or characters, each of them equally well executed, the one in prose and the other in verse, the verse will be read a hundred times where the prose is read once.

Having thus explained a few of my reasons for writing in verse, and why I have chosen subjects from common life, and endeavoured to bring my language near to the real language of men, if I have been too minute in pleading my own cause, I have at the same time been treating a subject of general interest ; and for this reason a few words shall be added with reference solely to these particular poems, and to some defects which will probably be found in them. I am sensible that my associations must have sometimes been particular instead of general, and that, consequently, giving to things a false importance, I may have sometimes written upon unworthy subjects ; but I am less apprehensive on this account, than that my language may frequently have suffered from those arbitrary connexions of feelings and ideas with particular words and phrases, from which no man can altogether protect himself. Hence I have no doubt, that, in some instances, feelings, even of the ludicrous, may be given to my Readers by expressions which appeared to me tender and pathetic. Such faulty expressions, were I convinced they were faulty at present, and that they must necessarily continue to be so, I would willingly take all reasonable pains to correct. But it is dangerous to make these alterations on the simple authority of a few individuals or even of certain classes of men ; for where the understanding of an Author is not convinced, or his feelings altered, this cannot be done without great injury to himself : for his own feelings are his stay and support ; and, if he set 10 them aside in one instance, he may be induced to repeat this act till his mind shall lose all confidence in itself, and become utterly debilitated. To this it may be added, that the Critic ought never to forget that he is himself exposed to the same errors as the Poet, and, perhaps, in a much greater degree : for there can be no presumption in saying of most readers, that it is not probable they will be so well acquainted with the various stages of meaning through which words have passed, or with the fickleness or stability of the relations of particular ideas to each other ; and, above all, since they 20 are so much less interested in the subject, they may decide lightly and carelessly.

Long as the Reader has been detained, I hope he will permit me to caution him against a mode of false criticism which has been applied to Poetry, in which the language closely resembles that of life and nature. Such verses have been triumphed over in parodies, of which Dr. Johnson's stanza is a fair specimen :—

> I put my hat upon my head,
> And walked into the Strand,   30
> And there I met another man
> Whose hat was in his hand.

Immediately under these lines let us place one of the most justly admired stanzas of the ' Babes in the Wood '.

These pretty Babes with hand in hand
Went wandering up and down;
But never more they saw the Man
Approaching from the Town.

In both these stanzas the words, and the order of the
words, in no respect differ from the most unimpassioned
conversation.   There are words in both, for example, ' the
Strand,' and ' the Town,' connected with none but the
most familiar ideas ; yet the one stanza we admit as admir-
10 able, and the other as a fair example of the superlatively
contemptible.   Whence arises this difference ?   Not from
the metre, not from the language, not from the order of the
words ; but the *matter* expressed in Dr. Johnson's stanza is
contemptible.   The proper method of treating trivial and
simple verses, to which Dr. Johnson's stanza would be
a fair parallelism, is not to say, this is a bad kind of poetry,
or, this is not poetry; but, this wants sense; it is neither
interesting in itself, nor can *lead* to anything interesting ;
the images neither originate in that sane state of feeling
20 which arises out of thought, nor can excite thought or feeling
in the Reader.   This is the only sensible manner of dealing
with such verses.   Why trouble yourself about the species
till you have previously decided upon the genus ?   Why
take pains to prove that an ape is not a Newton, when it is
self-evident that he is not a man ?

One request I must make of my reader, which is, that in
judging these Poems he would decide by his own feelings
genuinely, and not by reflection upon what will probably
be the judgement of others.   How common is it to hear
30 a person say, I myself do not object to this style of composition, or this or that expression, but, to such and such
classes of people it will appear mean or ludicrous!   This mode
of criticism, so destructive of all sound unadulterated judgement, is almost universal : let the Reader then abide, inde-
pendently, by his own feelings, and, if he finds himself

affected, let him not suffer such conjectures to interfere with his pleasure.

If an Author, by any single composition, has impressed us with respect for his talents, it is useful to consider this as affording a presumption, that on other occasions where we have been displeased, he, nevertheless, may not have written ill or absurdly ; and further, to give him so much credit for this one composition as may induce us to review what has displeased us, with more care than we should otherwise have bestowed upon it. This is not only an act of justice, but, in 10 our decisions upon poetry especially, may conduce, in a high degree, to the improvement of our own taste ; for an *accurate* taste in poetry, and in all the other arts, as Sir Joshua Reynolds has observed, is an *acquired* talent, which can only be produced by thought and a long continued intercourse with the best models of composition. This is mentioned, not with so ridiculous a purpose as to prevent the most inexperienced Reader from judging for himself (I have already said that I wish him to judge for himself), but merely to temper the rashness of decision, and to suggest, that, if 20 Poetry be a subject on which much time has not been bestowed, the judgement may be erroneous ; and that, in many cases, it necessarily will be so.

Nothing would, I know, have so effectually contributed to further the end which I have in view, as to have shown of what kind the pleasure is, and how that pleasure is produced, which is confessedly produced by metrical composition essentially different from that which I have here endeavoured to recommend : for the Reader will say that he has been pleased by such composition ; and what more 30 can be done for him ? The power of any art is limited ; and he will suspect, that, if it be proposed to furnish him with new friends, that can be only upon condition of his abandoning his old friends. Besides, as I have said, the Reader is himself conscious of the pleasure which he has received from such composition, composition to which he has peculiarly attached the endearing name of Poetry ; and all men feel an habitual gratitude, and something of an honourable bigotry, for the objects which have long continued to please them : we not only wish to be pleased, but to be pleased in that particular way in which we have been accustomed to be pleased. There is in these feelings enough to resist a host of arguments ; and I should be the less able to combat them successfully, as I am willing to allow that, in order entirely to enjoy the Poetry which I am recommending, it would be necessary to give up much of what is ordinarily enjoyed. But, would my limits have permitted me to point out how this pleasure is produced, many obstacles might have been removed, and the Reader assisted in perceiving that the powers of language are not so limited as he may suppose ; and that it is possible for poetry to give other enjoyments, of a purer, more lasting, and more exquisite nature. This part of the subject has not been altogether neglected, but it has not been so much my present aim to prove, that the interest excited by some other kinds of poetry is less vivid, and less worthy of the nobler powers of the mind, as to offer reasons for presuming, that if my purpose were fulfilled, a species of poetry would be produced, which is genuine poetry ; in its nature well adapted to interest mankind permanently, and likewise important in the multiplicity and quality of its moral relations.

From what has been said, and from a perusal of the Poems, the Reader will be able clearly to perceive the object which I had in view : he will determine how far it has been attained ; and, what is a much more important question, whether it be worth attaining : and upon the decision of these two questions will rest my claim to the approbation of the Public.

LETTER

TO

LADY BEAUMONT

Coleorton, May 21, 1807.

MY DEAR LADY BEAUMONT,

Though I am to see you so soon, I cannot but write a word or two, to thank you for the interest you take in my poems, as evinced by your solicitude about their immediate reception. I write partly to thank you for this, and to express the pleasure it has given me, and partly to remove any uneasiness from your mind which the disappointments you sometimes meet with, in this labour of love, may occasion. I see that you have many battles to fight for me,—more than, in the ardour and confidence of your pure and elevated 10 mind, you had ever thought of being summoned to ; but be assured that this opposition is nothing more than what I distinctly foresaw that you and my other friends would have to encounter. I say this, not to give myself credit for an eye of prophecy, but to allay any vexatious thoughts on my account which this opposition may have produced in you.

It is impossible that any expectations can be lower than mine concerning the immediate effect of this little work upon what is called the public. I do not here take into consideration the envy and malevolence, and all the bad 20 passions which always stand in the way of a work of any merit from a living poet ; but merely think of the pure, absolute, honest ignorance in which all worldlings of every rank and situation must be enveloped, with respect to the thoughts, feelings, and images, on which the life of my poems depends. The things which I have taken, whether from within or without, what have they to do with routs, dinners, morning calls, hurry from door to door, from street to street, on foot or in carriage ; with Mr. Pitt or Mr. Fox, Mr. Paul or Sir Francis Burdett, the Westminster election or the borough of Honiton ? In a word—for I cannot stop to make my way through the hurry of images that present themselves to me—what have they to do with endless talking about things nobody cares anything for except as far as their own vanity is concerned, and this with persons they 10 care nothing for but as their vanity or *selfishness* is concerned ?—what have they to do (to say all at once) with a life without love ? In such a life there can be no thought ; for we have no thought (save thoughts of pain) but as far as we have love and admiration.

It is an awful truth, that there neither is, nor can be, any genuine enjoyment of poetry among nineteen out of twenty of those persons who live, or wish to live, in the broad light of the world—among those who either are, or are striving to make themselves, people of consideration in society.   This 20 is a truth, and an awful one, because to be incapable of a feeling of poetry, in my sense of the word, is to be without love of human nature and reverence for God.

Upon this I shall insist elsewhere ; at present let me confine myself to my object, which is to make you, my dear friend, as easy-hearted as myself with respect to these poems.   Trouble not yourself upon their present reception ; of what moment is that compared with what I trust is their destiny ?—to console the afflicted ; to add sunshine to daylight, by making the happy happier ; to teach the young 30 and the gracious of every age to see, to think, and feel, and, therefore, to become more actively and securely virtuous ; this is their office, which I trust they will faithfully perform, long after we (that is, all that is mortal of us) are mouldered in our graves.   I am well aware how far it would seem to many I overrate my own exertions, when I speak in this way, in direct connexion with the volume I have just made public.

I am not, however, afraid of such censure, insignificant as probably the majority of those poems would appear to very respectable persons. I do not mean London wits and witlings, for these have too many foul passions about them to be respectable, even if they had more intellect than the benign laws of Providence will allow to such a heartless existence as theirs is ; but grave, kindly-natured, worthy persons, who would be pleased if they could. I hope that these volumes are not without some recommendations, even for readers of this class : but their imagination has slept ; and the voice which is the voice of my poetry, without imagination, cannot be heard. Leaving these, I was going to say a word to such readers as Mr. ——. Such !—how would he be offended if he knew I considered him only as a representative of a class, and not an unique ! ' Pity,' says Mr. ——, ' that so many trifling things should be admitted to obstruct the view of those that have merit.' Now, let this candid judge take, by way of example, the sonnets, which, probably, with the exception of two or three other poems, for which I will not contend, appear to him the most trifling, as they are the shortest. I would say to him, omitting things of higher consideration, there is one thing which must strike you at once, if you will only read these poems,—that those ' to Liberty ', at least, have a connexion with, or a bearing upon, each other ; and, therefore, if individually they want weight, perhaps, as a body, they may not be so deficient. At least, this ought to induce you to suspend your judgement, and qualify it so far as to allow that the writer aims at least at comprehensiveness.

But, dropping this, I would boldly say at once, that these sonnets, while they each fix the attention upon some important sentiment, separately considered, do, at the same time, collectively make a poem on the subject of civil liberty

and national independence, which, either for simplicity of
style or grandeur of moral sentiment, is, alas ! likely to have
few parallels in the poetry of the present day. Again, turn
to the ' Moods of my own Mind.'   There is scarcely a poem
here of above thirty lines, and very trifling these poems will
appear to many ; but, omitting to speak of them individually, do they not, taken collectively, fix the attention
upon a subject eminently poetical, viz., the interest which
objects in nature derive from the predominance of certain
10 affections, more or less permanent, more or less capable of
salutary renewal in the mind of the being contemplating
these objects ? This is poetic, and essentially poetic. And
why ? Because it is creative.

   .   .   .   .

My letter (as this second sheet, which I am obliged to take
admonishes me) is growing to an enormous length ; and yet,
saving that I have expressed my calm confidence that these
poems will live, I have said nothing which has a particular
application to the object of it, which was to remove all disquiet from your mind on account of the condemnation they
20 may at present incur from that portion of my contemporaries who are called the public. I am sure, my dear Lady
Beaumont, if you attach any importance to it, it can only
be from an apprehension that it may affect me, upon which
I have already set you at ease ; or from a fear that this
present blame is ominous of their future or final destiny. If
this be the case, your tenderness for me betrays you. Be
assured that the decision of these persons has nothing to do
with the question ; they are altogether incompetent judges.
These people, in the senseless hurry of their idle lives, do not
30 *read* books, they merely snatch a glance at them, that they
may talk about them.   And even if this were not so, never
forget what, I believe, was observed to you by Coleridge,
that every great and original writer, in proportion as he is
great or original, must himself create the taste by which he

is to be relished ; he must teach the art by which he is to be seen ; this, in a certain degree, even to all persons, however wise and pure may be their lives, and however unvitiated their taste.   But for those who dip into books in order to give an opinion of them, or talk about them to take up an opinion—for this multitude of unhappy, and misguided, and misguiding beings, an entire regeneration must be produced ; and if this be possible, it must be a work *of time.* To conclude, my ears are stone-dead to this idle buzz, and my flesh as insensible as iron to these petty stings ; and, 10 after what I have said, I am sure yours will be the same.   I doubt not that you will share with me an invincible confidence that my writings (and among them these little poems) will co-operate with the benign tendencies in human nature and society, wherever found ; and that they will, in their degree, be efficacious in making men wiser, better, and happier.   Farewell !   I will not apologize for this letter, though its length demands an apology.   Believe me, eagerly wishing for the happy day when I shall see you and Sir George here,

Most affectionately yours,
W. WORDSWORTH.

From the Tract on
THE CONVENTION OF CINTRA

TALK not of the perishable nature of enthusiasm; and rise above a craving for perpetual manifestations of things. He is to be pitied whose eye can only be pierced by the light of a meridian sun, whose frame can only be warmed by the heat of mid-summer. Let us hear no more of the little dependence to be had in war upon voluntary service. The things with which we are primarily and mainly concerned are inward passions, and not outward arrangements. These latter may be given 10 at any time, when the parts to be put together are in readiness. Hatred and love, and each in its intensity, and pride (passions which, existing in the heart of a Nation, are inseparable from hope)—these elements being in constant preparation, enthusiasm will break out from them, or coalesce with them, upon the summons of a moment. And these passions are scarcely less than inextinguishable. The truth of this is recorded in the manners and hearts of North and South Britons, of Englishmen and Welshmen, on either border of the Tweed and of the Esk, 20 on both sides of the Severn and the Dee; an inscription legible, and in strong characters, which the tread of many and great blessings, continued through hundreds of years, has been unable to efface. The Sicilian Vespers are to this day a familiar game among the boys of the villages on the sides of Mount Etna, and through every corner of the Island; and 'Exterminate the French!' is the action in their arms, and the word of triumph upon their tongues. He then is a sorry Statist, who desponds or despairs (nor is he less so who is too much elevated)

from any considerations connected with the quality of
enthusiasm. Nothing is so easy as to sustain it by partial
and gradual changes of its object, and by placing it in
the way of receiving new interpositions according to the
need. The difficulty lies—not in kindling, feeding, or
fanning the flame ; but in continuing so to regulate the
relations of things that the fanning breeze and the
feeding fuel shall come from no unworthy quarter, and
shall neither of them be wanting in appropriate consecration. The Spaniards have as great helps towards 10
ensuring this, as ever were vouchsafed to a People.

What then is to be desired ? Nothing but that the
Government and the higher orders of society should
deal sincerely towards the middle class and the lower :
I mean, that the general temper should be sincere. It
is not required that every one should be disinterested,
or zealous, or of one mind with his fellows. Selfishness
or slackness in individuals, and in certain bodies of men
also (and at times perhaps in all), have their use : else
why should they exist ? Due circumspection and necessary 20
activity, in those who are sound, could not otherwise
maintain themselves. The deficiencies in one quarter
are more than made up by consequent overflowings in
another. ' If my Neighbour fails,' says the true Patriot,
' more devolves upon me.' Discord and even treason
are not, in a country situated as Spain is, the pure evils
which, upon a superficial view, they appear to be. Never
are a people so livelily admonished of the love they bear
their country, and of the pride which they have in their
common parent, as when they hear of some parricidal 30
attempt of a false brother. For this cause chiefly, in
times of national danger, are their fancies so busy in
suspicion ; which under such shape, though oftentimes
producing dire and pitiable effects, is notwithstanding
in its general character no other than that habit which

has grown out of the instinct of self-preservation—elevated into a wakeful and affectionate apprehension for the whole, and ennobling its private and baser ways by the generous use to which they are converted. Nor ever has a good and loyal man such a swell of mind, such a clear insight into the constitution of virtue, and such a sublime sense of its power, as at the first tidings of some atrocious act of perfidy; when, having taken the alarm for human nature, a second thought recovers him; and his faith returns—gladsome from what has been revealed within himself, and awful from participation of the secrets in the profaner grove of humanity which that momentary blast laid open to his view.

Of the ultimate independence of the Spanish Nation there is no reason to doubt: and for the immediate furtherance of the good cause, and a throwing-off of the yoke upon the first favourable opportunity by the different tracts of the country upon which it has been re-imposed, nothing is wanting but sincerity on the part of the government towards the provinces which are yet free. The first end to be secured by Spain is riddance of the enemy: the second, permanent independence: and the third, a free constitution of government; which will give their main (though far from sole) value to the other two; and without which little more than a formal independence, and perhaps scarcely that, can be secured. Humanity and honour, and justice, and all the sacred feelings connected with atonement, retribution, and satisfaction; shame that will not sleep, and the sting of unperformed duty; and all the powers of the mind, the memory that broods over the dead and turns to the living, the understanding, the imagination, and the reason;—demand and enjoin that the wanton oppressor should be driven, with confusion and dismay, from the country which he has so heinously abused. . . .

There is yet another case in which a People may be benefited by resignation or forfeiture of their rights as a separate independent State ; I mean, where—of two contiguous or neighbouring countries, both included by nature under one conspicuously defined limit—the weaker is united with, or absorbed into, the more powerful ; and one and the same Government is extended over both. This, with due patience and foresight, may (for the most part) be amicably effected, without the intervention of conquest ; but even should a violent course have been resorted to, and have proved successful, the result will be matter of congratulation rather than of regret, if the countries have been incorporated with an equitable participation of natural advantages and civil privileges. Who does not rejoice that former partitions have disappeared,— and that England, Scotland, and Wales, are under one legislative and executive authority ; and that Ireland (would that she had been more justly dealt with !) follows the same destiny ?   The large and numerous Fiefs, which interfered injuriously with the grand demarcation assigned by nature to France, have long since been united and consolidated.   The several independent Sovereignties of Italy (a country, the boundary of which is still more expressly traced out by nature ; and which has no less the further definition and cement of country which Language prepares) have yet this good to aim at : and it will be a happy day for Europe, when the natives of Italy and the natives of Germany (whose duty is, in like manner, indicated to them) shall each dissolve the pernicious barriers which divide them, and form themselves into a mighty people.   But Spain, excepting a free union with Portugal, has no benefit of this kind to look for : she has long since attained it.   The Pyrenees on the one side, and the Sea on every other ;   the vast extent and great resources of the territory ;   a population numerous enough

to defend itself against the whole world, and capable of
great increase ; language; and long duration of independence ;—point out and command that the two nations of the
Peninsula should be united in friendship and strict alliance ;
and, as soon as it may be effected without injustice, form
one independent and indissoluble sovereignty. The
Peninsula cannot be protected but by itself : it is too
large a tree to be framed by nature for a station among
underwoods ; it must have power to toss its branches
10 in the wind, and lift a bold forehead to the sun. . . .

There are multitudes by whom, I know, these sentiments
will not be languidly received at this day ; and sure I
am that, a hundred and fifty years ago, they would
have been ardently welcomed by all. But, in many
parts of Europe (and especially in our own country), men
have been pressing forward, for some time, in a path
which has betrayed by its fruitfulness ; furnishing them
constant employment for picking up things about their
feet, when thoughts were perishing in their minds. While
20 Mechanic Arts, Manufactures, Agriculture, Commerce,
and all those products of knowledge which are confined
to gross, definite, and tangible objects, have, with
the aid of Experimental Philosophy, been every day
putting on more brilliant colours ; the splendour of the
Imagination has been fading : Sensibility, which was
formerly a generous nursling of rude Nature, has been
chased from its ancient range in the wide domain of
patriotism and religion with the weapons of derision by
a shadow calling itself Good Sense : calculations of pre-
30 sumptuous Expediency, groping its way among partial
and temporary consequences, have been substituted
for the dictates of paramount and infallible Conscience,
the supreme embracer of consequences : lifeless and
circumspect Decencies have banished the graceful negli-
gence and unsuspicious dignity of Virtue.

The progress of these arts also, by furnishing such attractive stores of outward accommodation, has misled the higher orders of society in their more disinterested exertions for the service of the lower. Animal comforts have been rejoiced over, as if they were the end of being. A neater and more fertile garden ; a greener field ; implements and utensils more apt ; a dwelling more commodious and better furnished ; let these be attained, say the actively benevolent, and we are sure not only of being in the right road, but of having successfully 10 terminated our journey. Now a country may advance, for some time, in this course with apparent profit : these accommodations, by zealous encouragement, may be attained : and still the Peasant or Artisan, their master, be a slave in mind ; a slave rendered even more abject by the very tenure under which these possessions are held : and if they veil from us this fact, or reconcile us to it, they are worse than worthless. The springs of emotion may be relaxed or destroyed within him ; he may have little thought of the past, and less interest 20 in the future.—The great end and difficulty of life for men of all classes, and especially difficult for those who live by manual labour, is a union of peace with innocent and laudable animation. Not by bread alone is the life of Man sustained ; not by raiment alone is he warmed ; —but by the genial and vernal inmate of the breast, which at once pushes forth and cherishes ; by self-support and self-sufficing endeavours ; by anticipations, apprehensions, and active remembrances ; by elasticity under insult, and firm resistance to injury ; by joy, and by 30 love ; by pride which his imagination gathers in from afar ; by patience, because life wants not promises ; by admiration ; by gratitude which—debasing him not when his fellow-being is its object—habitually expands itself, for his elevation, in complacency towards his Creator.

Now, to the existence of these blessings, national independence is indispensable ; and many of them it will itself produce and maintain. For it is some consolation to those who look back upon the history of the world to know that, even without civil liberty, society may possess—diffused through its inner recesses in the minds even of its humblest members—something of dignified enjoyment. But, without national independence, this is impossible. . . .

.   .   .   .

10   The Peasant, and he who lives by the fair reward of his manual labour, has ordinarily a larger proportion of his gratifications dependent upon these thoughts, than, for the most part, men in other classes have. For he is in his person attached, by stronger roots, to the soil of which he is the growth : his intellectual notices are generally confined within narrower bounds : in him no partial or antipatriotic interests counteract the force of those nobler sympathies and antipathies which he has in right of his Country : and lastly the belt or girdle
20 of his mind has never been stretched to utter relaxation by false philosophy, under a conceit of making it sit more easily and gracefully. These sensations are a social inheritance to him ; more important, as he is precluded from luxurious, and those which are usually called refined, enjoyments.

THE CLIMATE
OF THE LAKE DISTRICT

From *A Guide through the District of the Lakes in the North of England*

It may now be proper to say a few words respecting climate, and 'skiey influences', in which this region, as far as the character of its landscapes is affected by them, may, upon the whole, be considered fortunate. The country is, indeed, subject to much bad weather, and it has been ascertained that twice as much rain falls here as in many parts of the island; but the number of black drizzling days, that blot out the face of things, is by no means *proportionally* great. Nor is a continuance of thick, flagging, damp air so common as in the West of England and Ireland. The rain here comes down heartily, and is frequently succeeded by clear, bright weather, when every brook is vocal, and every torrent sonorous; brooks and torrents, which are never muddy, even in the heaviest floods, except, after a drought, they happen to be defiled for a short time by waters that have swept along dusty roads, or have broken out into ploughed fields. Days of unsettled weather, with partial showers, are very frequent; but the showers, darkening, or brightening, as they fly from hill to hill, are not less grateful to the eye than finely interwoven passages of gay and sad music are touching to the ear. Vapours exhaling from the lakes and meadows after sunrise, in a hot season, or, in moist weather, brooding upon the heights, or descending towards the valleys with inaudible motion, give a visionary character to everything around them; and are in themselves so beautiful, as to dispose us to enter into the feelings of those simple nations (such as the Laplanders of this day) by whom they are taken for

guardian deities of the mountains; or to sympathize with others who have fancied these delicate apparitions to be the spirits of their departed ancestors. Akin to these are fleecy clouds resting upon the hill-tops; they are not easily managed in picture, with their accompaniments of blue sky; but how glorious are they in Nature! how pregnant with imagination for the poet! and the height of the Cumbrian mountains is sufficient to exhibit daily and hourly instances of those mysterious attach-
10 ments. Such clouds, cleaving to their stations, or lifting up suddenly their glittering heads from behind rocky barriers, or hurrying out of sight with speed of the sharpest edge, will often tempt an inhabitant to congratulate himself on belonging to a country of mists and clouds and storms, and make him think of the blank sky of Egypt, and of the cerulean vacancy of Italy, as an unanimated and even a sad spectacle. The atmosphere, however, as in every country subject to much rain, is frequently unfavourable to landscape, especially when keen winds
20 succeed the rain, which are apt to produce coldness, spottiness, and an unmeaning or repulsive detail in the distance; —a sunless frost, under a canopy of leaden and shapeless clouds, is, as far as it allows things to be seen, equally disagreeable.

It has been said that in human life there are moments worth ages. In a more subdued tone of sympathy may we affirm, that in the climate of England there are, for the lover of Nature, days which are worth whole months, —I might say—even years. One of these favoured days
30 sometimes occurs in spring-time, when that soft air is breathing over the blossoms and new-born verdure, which inspired Buchanan with his beautiful Ode to the first of May; the air, which, in the luxuriance of his fancy, he likens to that of the golden age,—to that which gives motion to the funereal cypresses on the banks of Lethe :—

to the air which is to salute beatified spirits when ex-
piatory fires shall have consumed the earth with all her
habitations. But it is in autumn that days of such affecting influence most frequently intervene ;—the atmosphere
seems refined, and the sky rendered more crystalline,
as the vivifying heat of the year abates ; the lights and
shadows are more delicate ; the colouring is richer and
more finely harmonized ; and, in this season of stillness,
the ear being unoccupied, or only gently excited, the
sense of vision becomes more susceptible of its appropriate 10
enjoyments. A resident in a country like this which we
are treating of, will agree with me, that the presence of
a lake is indispensable to exhibit in perfection the beauty
of one of these days ; and he must have experienced,
while looking on the unruffled waters, that the imagination, by their aid, is carried into recesses of feeling otherwise impenetrable. The reason of this is, that the heavens
are not only brought down into the bosom of the earth,
but that the earth is mainly looked at, and thought of,
through the medium of a purer element. The happiest 20
time is when the equinoxial gales are departed ; but
their fury may probably be called to mind by the sight
of a few shattered boughs, whose leaves do not differ
in colour from the faded foliage of the stately oaks from
which these relics of the storm depend : all else speaks
of tranquillity ;—not a breath of air, no restlessness of
insects, and not a moving object perceptible—except
the clouds gliding in the depths of the lake, or the traveller
passing along, an inverted image, whose motion seems
governed by the quiet of a time, to which its archetype, 30
the living person, is, perhaps, insensible :—or it may
happen, that the figure of one of the larger birds, a raven
or a heron, is crossing silently among the reflected clouds,
while the voice of the real bird, from the element aloft,
gently awakens in the spectator the recollection of appetites

and instincts, pursuits and occupations, that deform and agitate the world,—yet have no power to prevent Nature from putting on an aspect capable of satisfying the most intense cravings for the tranquil, the lovely, and the perfect, to which man, the noblest of her creatures, is subject.

NOTES

COLERIDGE ON WORDSWORTH

THIS is a portion of the twenty-second chapter of Coleridge's *Biographia Literaria*, 1817. Coleridge took the quotations from the 1815 edition of Wordsworth's poems.

PAGE 1, l. 6. *I have already expressed*, in earlier chapters of the *Biographia Literaria*, notably iv, xiv, xvii-xx.

l. 22. *Cowley's Essay on Cromwell,—A Discourse by way of Vision concerning the Government of Oliver Cromwell*, 1661, by Abraham Cowley (1618–1667).

l. 24. *the Consolation of Boetius*. The treatise on the *Consolation of Philosophy* was composed by Boetius (A.D. *c.* 470–524) while awaiting execution on a false charge of treason to his master Theodoric.

the Argenis, a didactic political romance in Latin by John Barclay (1582–1621). A copy of the English translation by Le Grys and Thomas May, 1629, with manuscript notes by Coleridge, is in the British Museum.

PAGE 2, l. 8. *Metastasio*, Pietro (1698–1782), Italian dramatist, who wrote for the operatic stage.

PAGE 3, l. 3. *Close by a pond*, &c. The stanza which concluded with these five lines was cancelled by Wordsworth in the edition of 1820 as a result of Coleridge's criticism. It came between stanzas viii and ix, p. 90.

PAGE 4, l. 25. *Aristotle pronounces*, in the *Poetics*, ix.

l. 29. *Davenant's prefatory letter to Hobbs*,—Sir William Davenant's preface to *Gondibert*, 1650, addressed ' to his much honour'd friend Mr. Hobbes ', the author of *Leviathan*.

PAGE 6, l. 18. *the head of Memnon*. Memnon was a legendary prince of Aethiopia who was slain by Achilles before Troy. The Greeks gave his name to the colossal statue near Thebes in Egypt which was fabled to give forth a sound like the snapping of a harp string when touched by the first rays of the sun.

l. 27. *his objectors*, notably Francis Jeffrey in his review of *The Excursion* in *The Edinburgh Review* for November 1814.

PAGE 8, l. 5. *Hysteron-Proteron*, i. e. the last first, an inversion of the actual or logical order.

l. 16. *Antonine*, Marcus Aurelius Antoninus (A.D. 121–180), Roman emperor (161–180) and philosopher.

l. 17. *Epictetus* (A.D. *c.* 60–*c.* 120) the Stoic, was a freed slave.

l. 18. *and rejoice*, &c. *The Excursion*, i. 75.

PAGE 8, l. 22. *O many are the poets*, &c. *The Excursion*, i. 77–93 (five lines omitted).

PAGE 9, l. 20. *I think of Chatterton*, &c. *Resolution and Independence*, 43–46, p. 89, purposely altered.

PAGE 10, l. 4. *precepts of Horace*, in the *Ars Poetica*, 119 ff.

PAGE 11, l. 5. *Hercules* took service with Omphale, queen of Lydia, on the prompting of an oracle, and span wool for her.

l. 14. *They flash*, &c.,—the daffodils, in ' I wandered lonely as a cloud', p. 100.

l. 28. *Thou best philosopher*, &c. *Ode on the Intimations of Immortality*, viii, p. 115. The line ' In darkness lost, the darkness of the grave ' was not in the editions of 1807 and 1815, but was added in 1820, when the four lines on p. 13 ' To whom . . . lie ' were omitted.

PAGE 12, l. 27. *Golconda*, the old name of Hyderabad, represented in the legends of travel as a gold-field of marvellous richness.

PAGE 14, l. 23. *Mr. Bowles*, William Lisle Bowles (1762–1850), whose Sonnets had ' delighted and inspired ' Coleridge in his school-days : see *Biographia Literaria*, chap. i.

l. 24. *laurel-honouring Laureate*, Robert Southey, Poet-Laureate from 1813 to 1843.

PAGE 15, l. 3. *Makes audible*, &c. Coleridge quotes from his own Lines *To a Gentleman* (i. e. Wordsworth).

l. 11. *O Reader !* &c. This and the next extract are from *Simon Lee*.

l. 20. *six beautiful quatrains* : from *The Fountain*, see p. 63.

PAGE 16, l. 9. *the sonnet on Buonaparte*. See p. 140.

l. 11. *the withered Celandine*. See p. 101.

l. 17. *Samuel Daniel* (1562–1619), author of ' Sonnets to Delia ', *Musophilus*, *The Civile Wars between the two houses of Lancaster and Yorke*, and numerous masques, was one of Wordsworth's favourite poets. Wordsworth occasionally incorporates lines or phrases from Daniel in his own poems. See p. 115, l. 103, p. 144, l. 4, and *The Excursion*, iv. 324–31.

PAGE 17, l. 3. *Fit audience*. *Paradise Lost*, vii. 31.

l. 27. *curiosa felicitas*, a phrase applied to Horace by Petronius Arbiter, *Satyricon*, lxxviii.

PAGE 18, l. 12. *description of skating*. See p. 66.

l. 23. *poem on the green linnet*. See p. 96. Wordsworth confessed that the last stanza as here given was ' very faulty ', and altered it so as to get rid of the word *teems* (a provincialism) and of *train* as applied to leaves.

PAGE 19, l. 5. *description of the blue-cap*,—in *The Kitten and Falling Leaves*.

l. 6. *poem to the cuckoo*. See p. 95.

l. 9. *Three years she grew*, &c. See p. 71.

l. 25. *Imagination . . . Fancy*. This was a distinction of great importance to Coleridge and to Wordsworth, who devoted several pages of his preface to the edition of 1815 to elucidating it. Imagination is the faculty that ' carries ' the object ' into the heart ' and endows it with a new life and quality, while Fancy plays with superficial resemblances between things. *Resolution and Independence* is classed by Wordsworth under the first faculty, and *To the Daisy* under the second.

PAGE 20, l. 3. *add the gleam*, &c. See p. 106, *Elegiac Stanzas*, 14–16.

PAGE 21, l. 4. Coleridge refers to the six sonnets beginning ' Where lies the Land to which yon Ship must go ', ' Even as a dragon's eye ', ' O Mountain Stream ! the Shepherd and his Cot ', ' Earth has not anything to show more fair ' (p. 140), ' Methought I saw the footsteps of a throne ', and ' It is a beauteous evening, calm and free ' (p. 141).

l. 5. *Subjugation of Switzerland.* See p. 145.

l. 8. *Bartram's Travels,—Travels thro' North and South Carolina and the Cherokee Country*, by W. Bartram, 1792, p. 36.

PAGE 22, l. 24. *Goody Blake*—in *Goody Blake and Harry Gill*; *Johnny and Betty Foy*—in *The Idiot Boy.*

HAZLITT ON WORDSWORTH

This is Hazlitt's essay on Wordsworth in *The Spirit of the Age*, 1825, a series of sketches of representative men of the time. He had reviewed *The Excursion* in two articles in *The Examiner* in August, 1814 (reprinted in *The Round Table*, 1817), and he had devoted part of two lectures to Wordsworth in his *Lectures on the English Poets*, 1818. He had also spoken of him occasionally, as in his essay ' On Genius and Common Sense ' in *Table Talk*, 1821, and had given personal recollections in ' My first Acquaintance with Poets ' (published in *The Liberal*, 1823). They have all much in common, but the essay in *The Spirit of the Age*, which was the last to be written, is Hazlitt's completest and most judicial estimate of Wordsworth.

PAGE 23, l. 5. *lowliness is young ambition's ladder,—Julius Caesar*, II. i. 22.

l. 9. *No figures nor no fantasies,*—Id. II. i. 231.

l. 23. *Skyey influences,—Measure for Measure*, III. i. 9.

l. 28. *Nihil humani*, &c. Terence, *Heautontimorumenos*, I. i. 25.

PAGE 24, l. 30. *the cloud-capt towers*, &c. *Tempest*, IV. i. 151–6.

PAGE 25, l. 4. *the judge's robe*, &c. *Measure for Measure*, II. ii. 59, 61.

l. 23. *a sense of joy*, &c. See *To My Sister*, p. 48.

l. 32. *Beneath the hills*, &c. *The Excursion*, vi. 553–7 (first line in ed. 1814 ' Amid the groves, beneath the shadowy hills '). Hazlitt generally quoted from memory.

PAGE **26**, l. 9. *vain pomp . . . hate ye. Henry VIII*, III. i. 366.

PAGE **27**, l. 5. *To him the meanest flower*, &c. *Intimations of Immortality*, last lines, p. 118.

ll. 7–14. *The daisy*, see p. 93 ; *the cuckoo*, see p. 95 ; *a linnet's nest*, apparently an allusion to *The Sparrow's Nest*, confused with *The Green Linnet*, p. 96 ; *an old withered thorn*, see *The Thorn* ; *a grey cloak*, see *Alice Fell* ; *the lichens on the rock*, see *The Thorn*, 11–13.

PAGE **28**, l. 20. *Cole-Orton*, in Leicestershire, the seat of Sir George Beaumont, a talented artist and a fast friend of Wordsworth from 1803 till his death in 1827. Wordsworth spent the winter of 1806–7 in a farm-house lent him by Beaumont. In the dedication to Beaumont of the 1815 edition of his Poems, Wordsworth says that ' several of the best pieces were composed under the shade of your own groves, upon the classic ground of Coleorton '.

l. 22. *lines on a Picture by Claude Lorraine*. Hazlitt refers to the sonnet entitled in 1815 merely *Upon the sight of a Beautiful Picture*. In later editions ' Painted by Sir G. H. Beaumont, Bart.' was added to the title, perhaps by way of correction of Hazlitt's error. The sonnet describes an Arcadian landscape, and of this kind of painting Claude was the great master. See p. 147.

l. 27. *Calm contemplation*, &c. See *Laodamia*, 72, p. 126.

PAGE **29**, l. 16. *Fall blunted*, &c. Goldsmith's *Traveller*, 232.

l. 20. *fit audience*, &c. *Paradise Lost*, vii. 31. Cf. the portion of *The Recluse* which Wordsworth published in 1814 in the preface to *The Excursion*, line 23, ' fit audience let me find though few ! '

PAGE **30**, l. 11. *toujours perdrix*. The allusion is to an old French tale which appears in the *Cent Nouvelles Nouvelles*, 1432. A king, reproached by his confessor for frequent lapses from conjugal fidelity, ordered his monitor to be served day after day with the favourite dish of his own choice, which was partridge.

l. 24. *man of no mark or likelihood—1 Henry IV*, III. ii. 45.

PAGE **31**, l. 27. *modernize some of the Canterbury Tales*. Hazlitt is here drawing on his recollections of Wordsworth's conversation, probably in 1803. When this essay was written, Wordsworth had published a modernized version of only one of the *Canterbury Tales*, the Prioress's—written 1801, published 1820. He had modernized about the same time the Manciple's Tale (*Memoirs of Wordsworth*, ii. 374), but he never published his version of it. He also modernized a portion of Chaucer's *Troilus and Cressida*, and *The Cuckoo and the Nightingale*, a fifteenth-century poem long attributed to Chaucer— both published in 1841. Cf. p. 153, foot-note.

PAGE **32**, l. 1. *interlocutions between Lucius and Caius*, in

Julius Caesar. This may be a recollection of Wordsworth's conversation.

l. 6. *Action is momentary*, &c. *The Borderers*, III. v. (1539–41). Wordsworth had read or recited these lines to Hazlitt (in 1798 ? or 1803 ?), and Hazlitt now quoted them from memory, not quite accurately, more than twenty years after he had heard them. *The Borderers*, written 1795-6, was not published till 1842, though these lines were printed with the dedication of *The White Doe of Rylstone* in 1837.

l. 11. *dislike to Gray.* Cf. *Preface to Lyrical Ballads*, p. 158. But he took Gray's *Ode to Adversity* as the model of his *Ode to Duty*.

l. 13. *Pope and Dryden.* Wordsworth's reply to this, in conversation, is recorded in his nephew's biography : ' I have been charged by some with disparaging Pope and Dryden. This is not so. I have committed much of both to memory. As far as Pope goes, he succeeds.'

l. 29. *Drawcansir,* a ' fierce Hero that does what he will without regard to good manners, justice, or numbers ' in *The Rehearsal*, 1672, a burlesque of the heroic dramas of Dryden and others, by the second Duke of Buckingham.

PAGE 33, l. 2. *Paley,* William (1743–1805), archdeacon of Carlisle, author of *Evidences of Christianity,* 1794.

l. 5. *Bewick,* Thomas (1753–1828), of Newcastle-upon-Tyne, wood-engraver, best known by his work for the *General History of Quadrupeds* and the *History of British Birds.*

Waterloo, Anthoine (1609–1662), engraver and etcher, who had a special fondness for forest scenery.

l. 8. *Nicolas Poussin* (1594–1665), perhaps the foremost master of the French School. Hazlitt has an essay ' On a Landscape of Nicolas Poussin ' in *Table-Talk.*

l. 25. *he hates conchology.* Hazlitt is quoting from the criticism of Wordsworth in his own *Lectures on the English Poets.*

l. 29. *Where one for sense,* &c. *Hudibras,* II. i. 29, 30.

PAGE 34, l. 14. *take the good,* &c. Dryden, *Alexander's Feast,* 106.

l. 22. *Lord Byron we have called,* &c., in the essay on Byron in *The Spirit of the Age.*

PAGE 35, l. 22. *God of his own idolatry.* Cf. *Romeo and Juliet,* II. ii. 114.

DE QUINCEY ON WORDSWORTH

This is the concluding portion of De Quincey's essay ' On Wordsworth's Poetry ', contributed to *Tait's Edinburgh Magazine* for September 1845. He had already written much about Wordsworth, in his ' Autobiography ' and ' Lake Reminiscences ' and elsewhere. In these he is mainly concerned with personal matters ; in the essay here quoted he confines himself to an examination of Wordsworth's poetry.

PAGE **36**, l. 4. *prevailed upon Coleridge*, &c.: ' I am sincerely glad that he has bidden farewell to all small poems, and is devoting himself to his great work [*The Prelude*]. . . . His only disease is the having been out of his element '—*Anima Poetae*. And see p. 21, ll. 17–20.

PAGE **37**, l. 16. *frozen by distance*. See *Address to Kilchurn Castle*, ll. 36–8 :

> Yon foaming flood seems motionless as ice ;
> Its dizzy turbulence eludes the eye,
> Frozen by distance.

Cf. ' stationary blasts of waterfalls ', *The Simplon Pass*, p. 68.
l. 23. *Twilight* . . . *its abstracting power*. See p. 148.
PAGE **38**, l. 23. *perplexing monarchs*. *Paradise Lost*, i. 599.
l. 33. *notice of it in Hesiod*. Nothing in Hesiod remotely resembles this line, but De Quincey may be thinking of Aratus, 938 f. Cf. Virgil, *Georgics*, i. 397, and Lucretius, vi. 504.

PAGE **39**, l. 1. *Another* . . . *in Lucan*. *Pharsalia*, i. 522.
l. 9. *Hamlet*, III. ii. 400.
l. 11. *Antony and Cleopatra*, IV. xii. 2.
l. 20. *Dampier*, William (1652–1715), pirate and discoverer, whose *Voyage round the World* was published in 1697.
l. 26. *Pope*. He is thinking of Pope's *Iliad*, viii. 687 ff. :

> As when the Moon, refulgent Lamp of Night !
> O'er Heav'ns clear Azure sheds her sacred Light, . . .
> Around her Throne the vivid Planets roll,
> And Stars unnumber'd gild the glowing Pole,
> O'er the dark Trees a yellower Verdure shed,
> And tip with Silver ev'ry Mountain's Head.

But he blunders in his recollection of it.

PAGE **40**, l. 19. *Excursion*, iv. 455 ff.
l. 20. *Hamilton Hills*, or ' Hambleton Hills ' ; see the sonnet beginning ' Dark and more dark the shades of evening fell '.
l. 21. *sky prospect*, &c. See *Memorials of a Tour on the Continent, 1820*, xxxiv (' Lo ! in the burning west, the craggy nape '). The lines quoted below are from this sonnet.

PAGE **41**, l. 6. *The cattle are grazing*, &c.,—from the poem headed ' Written in March, while resting on the Bridge at the Foot of Brother's Water ' and beginning ' The cock is crowing'.

PAGE **42**, l. 28. *Thoughts that do often lie*, &c. *Intimations of Immortality*, last line, p. 118.
l. 30. *The child is father*, &c. ' My heart leaps up,' p. 93
PAGE **43**, l. 3. *Foundations*, &c. *Malham Cove*, l. 10.
l. 30. *Forty and seven years*, from the publication of *Lyrical Ballads*. But Wordsworth had published *An Evening Walk* and *Descriptive Sketches* in 1793.

PAGE 46. REMEMBRANCE OF COLLINS

William Collins died in 1759 in his thirty-ninth year, worn out with trouble and a long disease of body and mind. One of his last poems (' later ditty ', l. 14) was his Ode to the memory of James Thomson, the author of *The Seasons*. Its scene ' is supposed to lie on the Thames near Richmond ', where Thomson died in 1748. Wordsworth had it continually in mind when writing these verses in ' Remembrance of Collins '; he took from it the words ' suspend the dashing oar '.

The poem was written while Wordsworth was an undergraduate at St. John's College, Cambridge.

PAGE 48. TO MY SISTER

l. 13. *Edward*, for ' Basil ', son of Wordsworth's college friend Basil Montagu. He was at this time five years of age and was living with the Wordsworths at Alfoxden.

PAGE 49. TINTERN ABBEY

' No poem of mine was composed under circumstances more pleasant for me to remember than this. I began it upon leaving Tintern, after crossing the Wye, and concluded it just as I was entering Bristol in the evening, after a ramble of four or five days (10th–13th July) with my sister. Not a line of it was altered, and not any part of it written down till I reached Bristol ' (Wordsworth, note dictated to Miss Fenwick).

l. 4. *soft inland murmur*. ' The river is not affected by the tides a few miles above Tintern ' (Wordsworth).

l. 106. *they half create*. Cf. Young's *Night Thoughts*, vi. 424 : ' And half-create the wondrous world they see.'

l. 115. These lines are addressed to his sister Dorothy ; cf. p. 48, *The Prelude*, xiv. 232 ff., and *The Sparrow's Nest*.

PAGE 54. THE OLD CUMBERLAND BEGGAR

' Observed, and with great benefit to my own heart, when I was a child. Written at Racedown and Alfoxden in my 28th year ' (Wordsworth).

l. 175. *chartered*, licensed to the office. Cf. *Ode to Duty*, l. 37.

PAGE 60. EXPOSTULATION AND REPLY

This and the following poem ' arose out of conversation with a friend who was somewhat unreasonably attached to modern books of moral philosophy ' (Advertisement to *Lyrical Ballads*, 1798). Mr. Thomas Hutchinson suggests that the friend may have been Hazlitt who, as we learn from his essay on ' My first Acquaintance with Poets ', had a metaphysical argument with Wordsworth during his visit to Coleridge at Nether Stowey in 1798. The poems were written about that time.

PAGE 62.   THE FOUNTAIN

One of a group sometimes called ' the Matthew Poems ', published 1800. Wordsworth said that this schoolmaster was ' made up of several, both of his class and men of other occupations '. In the main, the original was evidently his own schoolmaster at Hawkshead.

PAGE 65.   INFLUENCE OF NATURAL OBJECTS

These lines are from *The Prelude*, i. 401 ff.—one of four passages that were printed before the publication of the entire poem in 1850. *The Friend*, in which they were first published, was ' a literary, moral, and political weekly paper . . . conducted by S. T. Coleridge, of Grasmere, Westmorland '. It ran from June 1809 to March 1810.

Wordsworth attended the school at Hawkshead, on Esthwaite Water, to the west of Windermere, from his ninth to his eighteenth year (1778–87).

PAGE 67.   NUTTING

This was intended as part of *The Prelude*, but not included in it. ' Like most of my school-fellows I was an impassioned Nutter.'

l. 11. *frugal Dame*, Anne Tyson, with whom he lived when at school at Hawkshead ; cf. *The Prelude*, ii. 87.

PAGE 68.   THE SIMPLON PASS

Another passage from *The Prelude*, vi. 621 ff.

Wordsworth and his college friend Robert Jones traversed this pass in their walking tour through France and Switzerland during the summer vacation of 1790.

PAGE 69.   STRANGE FITS OF PASSION

This and the following four poems form a group known as ' the Lucy Poems '. They were all composed at Goslar in the Harz mountains. Wordsworth went to Germany with his sister Dorothy and Coleridge in September 1798 and returned with Dorothy in the following April. ' We have spent our time pleasantly enough in Germany,' he wrote in a letter, ' but we are right glad to find ourselves in England—for we have learnt to know its value.' Cf. ' I travelled among unknown men ', p. 70.

PAGE 73.   MICHAEL

' The character and circumstances of Luke were taken from a family to whom had belonged, many years before, the house we lived in at Town-end ' (Wordsworth). Wordsworth settled at Dove Cottage, Town-end, Grasmere, in December 1799.

l. 2. *Green-head Ghyll*, at the north-east of the vale of Grasmere. The remains of the sheepfold could be seen throughout Wordsworth's lifetime.

PAGE 88.   RESOLUTION AND INDEPENDENCE

'This old man I met a few hundred yards from my cottage at Town-end, Grasmere; and the account of him is taken from his own mouth' (Wordsworth).

The poem was originally named (before publication) *The Leech-Gatherer*.

l. 44. *perished in his pride.* Thomas Chatterton (1752–1770) took his own life in the despondency caused by the failure of his poetic ambition. His 'Rowley Poems', which he professed to have discovered in a fifteenth-century manuscript, were begun before he was twelve years old.

l. 45. *Him,* Robert Burns. Cf. p. 9.

PAGE 93.   TO THE DAISY

l. 3. *again.* This is one of three poems to the same flower written in 1802.

PAGE 98.   THE SOLITARY REAPER

Wordsworth said in a note that 'this Poem was suggested by a beautiful sentence in a MS. Tour in Scotland written by a Friend'. The reference is to Thomas Wilkinson's *Tours to the British Mountains,* published in 1824; and the words are: 'Passed a female, who was reaping alone: she sung in Erse, as she bended over her sickle; the sweetest human voice I ever heard: her strains were tenderly melancholy, and felt delicious long after they were heard no more.'

PAGE 99.   SHE WAS A PHANTOM OF DELIGHT

According to De Quincey (*Reminiscences of the Lake Poets,* ed. Masson, ii. 237) these lines were dedicated to Mrs. Wordsworth and were understood to describe her; 'hers they are, and will remain for ever.'

PAGE 100.   I WANDERED LONELY AS A CLOUD

The occasion of this poem is recorded by Dorothy Wordsworth in her *Journal* for April 15, 1802; she speaks of a long belt of daffodils, about the breadth of a country turnpike road, some of which 'tossed and reeled and danced, and seemed as if they verily laughed with the wind, that blew upon them over the lake'.

The second stanza was added in 1815, when 'golden' (l. 4) was substituted for 'dancing', and 'jocund' (l. 16) for 'laughing'.

ll. 21, 22. These two lines were by Mrs. Wordsworth. They were said by Wordsworth to be 'the two best lines in the poem'. Contrast Coleridge's criticism, p. 11.

PAGE 101.   THE SMALL CELANDINE

'What adds much to the interest that attends [this flower] is its habit of shutting itself up and opening out according to the degree of light and temperature of the air' (Wordsworth).

PAGE **102.**   THE FRENCH REVOLUTION

Another passage from *The Prelude*, xi. 105 ff.—first published by itself in Coleridge's *Friend* : cf. p. 65 note. See notes on Sonnets ' I grieved for Buonaparte ' (p. 140) and ' Inland within a hollow vale ' (p. 142).

PAGE **103.**   ODE TO DUTY

' This ode is on the model of Gray's Ode to Adversity, which is copied from Horace's Ode to Fortune ' (Wordsworth).

Many changes were made in the poem in successive editions. The most important was the omission of a stanza which is found only in the edition of 1807 :

> Yet not the less would I throughout
> Still act according to the voice
> Of my own wish ; and feel past doubt
> That my submissiveness was choice :
> Not seeking in the school of pride
> For ' precepts over dignified ',
> Denial and restraint I prize
> No farther than they breed a second Will more wise.

This was the sixth stanza, coming between ll. 40 and 41 of the final version.

l. 1.   *Stern Daughter.*   Cf. *Paradise Lost*, ix. 652 :

> God so commanded, and left that Command
> Sole Daughter of his voice.

l. 53.   *lowly wise.*   Cf. *Paradise Lost*, viii. 173.

PAGE **105.**   ELEGIAC STANZAS

Written in the summer of 1805, some months after the poet's sailor brother, John Wordsworth, had been drowned at sea. The Peele Castle of this poem is a little south of Barrow-in-Furness. The ' four summer weeks ' (l. 2) were passed at Rampside, a neighbouring village, probably in 1794. For Sir George Beaumont, see p. 196, note on p. 28, l. 20. An engraving of his picture forms the frontispiece to the 1815 edition of Wordsworth's Poems, vol. i.

ll. 14–16. In the edition of 1820 these lines, which may be misunderstood if taken out of their setting, were altered to

> and add a gleam
> Of lustre, known to neither sea nor land,
> But borrowed from the youthful Poet's dream.

They describe, not the revealing light of the imagination, but the colourings of fancy ; cf. the lines on ' many a gleam of fancy ' in *The Waggoner*, iv. 202.   ' The happiness that is to be coveted is the happiness of fearless vision, " and frequent sights of what is to be borne ".   And it is by the daylight of truth, not by " the light that never was on sea or land ", that the poet desires to look upon the things of earth ' (Raleigh, *Words-*

worth, pp. 107–9). The difficulty lies in the word ' consecration ', which is ' used, as it would seem, for a dream-like glory,
a peace attained by shunning reality '. Wordsworth restored
the original lines in 1832.

PAGE 108. CHARACTER OF THE HAPPY WARRIOR

Wordsworth stated in a note to this poem in 1807 that it
was ' written soon after tidings had been received of the
Death of Lord Nelson, which event directed the Author's
thoughts to the subject '. To this he added, in a note dictated
to Miss Fenwick towards the end of his life, that ' many
elements of the character here portrayed were found in my
brother John, who perished by shipwreck '. The *Ode to Duty*,
the *Elegiac Stanzas*, and *The Happy Warrior* were all inspired,
mainly or in part, by the memory of his brother. In a letter
to Sir George Beaumont written shortly after receiving news
of his brother's death he had said of him that ' of all human
beings whom I ever knew, he was the man of the most rational
desires, the most sedate habits, and the most perfect self-
command '.

l. 63. *approve*, give evidence of.

PAGE 110.   LOUD IS THE VALE !

Charles James Fox died on September 13, 1806.

l. 10. ' Importuna e grave salma.—Michael Angelo '
(Wordsworth).

PAGE 111.   INTIMATIONS OF IMMORTALITY

The first four stanzas of this poem appear to have been
written in the spring and summer of 1802 ; the remainder in
1805 or 1806, after his brother's death had pressed the question
of immortality on the poet's mind.

Wordsworth, in a long note given to Miss Fenwick, referring
to his inability during childhood to conceive the idea of death,
said : ' It was not so much from the source of animal vivacity
that *my* difficulty came as from a sense of the indomitableness
of the spirit within me. I used to brood over the stories of
Enoch and Elijah, and almost to persuade myself that, whatever might become of others, I should be translated in something of the same way to heaven. With a feeling congenial
to this, I was often unable to think of external things as
having external existence, and I communed with all that
I saw as something not apart from, but inherent in, my own
immaterial nature. Many times while going to school have
I grasped at a wall or tree to recall myself from this abyss of
idealism to the reality.' See ll. 145–51. We find him again
referring to this experience on an occasion recorded in a letter
by Bonamy Price (Oxford, April 21, 1881) printed in the
Transactions of the Wordsworth Society (1880–6), No. 2,

pp. **25, 26**: ' The venerable old man raised his aged form erect ; he was walking in the middle, and passed across me to a five-barred gate in the wall which bounded the road on the side of the lake [Rydal Water, by the sycamores under Nab Scar]. He clenched the top bar firmly with his right hand, pushed strongly against it, and then uttered these ever-memorable words : " There was a time in my life when I had to push against something that resisted, to be sure there was anything outside of me. I was sure of my own mind ; everything else fell away, and vanished into thought." Thought he was sure of ; matter for him, at the moment, was an unreality—nothing but a thought. Such natural spontaneous idealism has probably never been felt by any other man.'

Of the belief in the pre-existence of the soul he said : ' It is far too shadowy a notion to be recommended to faith as more than an element in our instincts of immortality. But let us bear in mind that, though the idea is not advanced in Revelation, there is nothing there to contradict it, and the fall of man presents an analogy in its favour. Accordingly a pre-existent state has entered into the popular creeds of many nations, and among all persons acquainted with classic literature is known as an ingredient in Platonic philosophy. [*Phaedrus*, 245–52 ; *Phaedo*, 73–7] . . . I took hold of the notion of pre-existence as having sufficient foundation in humanity for authorizing me to make for my purpose the best use of it I could as a Poet.'

l. **103**. ' *humorous stage* ', from Samuel Daniel's sonnet introductory to *Musophilus, containing a generall Defence of Learning* (1599) ; see note on p. 16, l. 17.

l. **110**. *Thou best philosopher*, &c. See Coleridge's criticism, p. 12.

ll. **121–4**. Omitted in 1820 and subsequently in deference to Coleridge's criticism, p. 13. See note on p. 11, l. 28.

PAGE **118**. SONG AT THE FEAST OF BROUGHAM CASTLE

The story of Henry Lord Clifford is told by Wordsworth in a note to this poem. His father, John Lord Clifford, was one of the principal champions of the House of Lancaster, and in the pursuit after Wakefield slew the boy Earl of Rutland, second son of the Duke of York. He fell at Towton, and his wife and infant son only escaped the vengeance of the enemy by flight and concealment. For twenty-four years the hero of this poem lived as a shepherd in Yorkshire or in Cumberland, near the estate of his father-in-law, Sir Lancelot Threlkeld. He was restored to his own after the battle of Bosworth (1485). It is recorded that ' when called to Parliament he behaved nobly and wisely ', but ' came seldom to London or the Court, and rather delighted to live in the

country ', and that he restored his decaying castles. Wordsworth mentions a tradition that during his life as a shepherd
he acquired much knowledge of astronomy. Of the places
mentioned in the poem, the Castles of Pendragon and Brough
near Appleby, that of Appleby itself on the banks of the Eden,
that of Brougham above the Emont, about two miles from
Penrith, and that of Skipton were in the hands of the Cliffords.
Blencathara was the ancient name of Saddleback ; Bowscale
Fell lies about two miles from Saddleback NNE., about midway
between it and Carrock Fell. Mosedale lies between the two
Fells. The Glenderamakin rises in Saddleback, and at first
flows NE. towards Mosedale. Threlkeld village is about four
miles from Keswick under the southern slope of Saddleback.

l. 122. *the undying fish.* A local legend attributed two
immortal fish to this tarn.

PAGE **124.**   LAODAMIA

Written in 1814 at Rydal Mount, where Wordsworth had
settled in 1813 and where he was to live the rest of his life.

This poem, like *Dion,* was the fruit of a renewed study of
the classics, undertaken with the immediate purpose of help-
ing his eldest son to prepare for the University. In the concluding note Wordsworth says that the character of Protesilaus
was suggested by the *Iphigenia in Aulis* of Euripides. But the
dominant influence throughout the poem was Virgil. ' It
cost me more trouble than almost anything of equal length
I have ever written.'

Protesilaus, the husband of Laodamia, was the first of the
Greeks to land on the soil of Troy, though he knew from the
oracle at Delphi that the first to land would be the first to
meet his death. He was slain by Hector. Laodamia beseeched
the Gods to restore him, and they restored him to her for
three hours.

l. 81. *Alcestis* died for her husband Admetus, king of Pherae
in Thessaly, the Gods having promised that he should escape
death if some one died in his stead. She was brought back
from the shades by Hercules.

l. 84. *Æson,* the father of Jason, excluded from the throne
of Iolcos in Thessaly by his brother Pelias. He was an infirm
old man when Jason returned from the Argonautic expedition,
but Medea's spells rejuvenated him.

ll. 158–63. This is the latest form of this stanza as given in
edd. 1845 and 1849. It was originally (edd. 1815 and 1820) as
follows :

> Ah, judge her gently who so deeply loved !
> Her, who, in reason's spite, yet without crime,
> Was in a trance of passion thus removed ;
> Delivered from the galling yoke of time
> And these frail elements—to gather flowers
> Of blissful quiet mid unfading bowers.

In ed. 1827 it was altered to:

> By no weak pity might the Gods be moved ;
> She who thus perished not without the crime
> Of Lovers that in Reason's spite have loved,
> Was doomed to wander in a grosser clime
> Apart from happy Ghosts—that gather flowers
> Of blissful quiet 'mid unfading bowers.

In edd. 1832 and 1836 l. 4 of this stanza became:

> Was doomed to wear out her appointed time.

In ed. 1840 ll. 1–3 became:

> She—who, though warned, exhorted, and reproved,
> Thus died, from passion desperate to a crime—
> By the just Gods, whom no weak pity moved,

Lines 4–6 were now in their final form. Lines 1–2 were given their final form (as in the text, p. 129) in ed. 1845.

These alterations illustrate Wordsworth's minute care—not always happily inspired, for he often reverted to earlier readings—in revising his work. They also show an important change in the motive of this poem. At first Laodamia is said to be ' without crime ' and is assigned to the realm of happy ghosts. Then she is excluded from this realm because she is ' not without crime ' in that she loved ' in reason's spite '. Finally she is excluded from it only for an ' appointed time '. Her sentence is reduced, but her error is not condoned. Why should Laodamia be dismissed to happiness in Elysium, Wordsworth argued, if she persisted in her immoderate passion and learned nothing from the counsel of Protesilaus ? And he cited Virgil as placing her among the unhappy ghosts of lovers (*Aeneid*, vi. 447). None the less the reader does not instinctively detect any miscarriage of justice in the fate he first assigned to her, and may regret that the original stanza was not ultimately restored. The poem as a whole is Wordsworth's most austere and majestic treatment of the tragic element in love—of love in conflict with reason and duty. Its teaching is summed up in these lines :

> the Gods approve
> The depth, and not the tumult, of the soul,
> A fervent, not ungovernable, love.

PAGE 130. EVENING OF EXTRAORDINARY SPLENDOUR

This is the last of Wordsworth's great visionary poems prompted by ' that blessed mood, in which . . . we see into the life of things ' ; and he was conscious when he wrote it that the gift which he had once possessed was now passed, and was only for the moment restored.

l. 73. *the light full early lost*, &c. Cf. *Intimations of Immortality*, ll. 66 ff., p, 113.

PAGE 133.   YARROW REVISITED

In September 1803 Wordsworth and his sister Dorothy, while on a tour in Scotland, passed close by the river Yarrow without turning aside to see it, partly from the feeling expressed in *Yarrow Unvisited* and in lines 77–80 of this poem. In 1814 in company with James Hogg, 'the Ettrick Shepherd', Wordsworth saw the river for the first time, and recorded the impression in *Yarrow Visited*. On September 21, 1831, he and his daughter paid a visit to Sir Walter Scott at Abbotsford, and on the following day Sir Walter took his guests on a visit to Newark. A few days later the 'Minstrel of the Border' left home for London on his way to Italy, in the vain search for health. He returned in July 1832, a dying man.

l. 2. *winsome Marrow*. From *The Braes of Yarrow*, by William Hamilton, of Bangour (1704–1754), beginning :

> Busk ye, busk ye, my bonny, bonny bride,
> Busk ye, busk ye, my winsome marrow.

This poem, 'in imitation of the ancient Scottish manner', was first printed in Allan Ramsay's *Tea-Table Miscellany*, 1724. ' Marrow ' means ' companion ', ' mate '.

l. 103. *last Minstrel*. See *The Lay of the Last Minstrel*, introduction.

PAGE 137.   DEATH OF JAMES HOGG

James Hogg, the Ettrick Shepherd, died November 21, 1835. Wordsworth wrote this note :

> Walter Scott died 21st Sept., 1832.
> S. T. Coleridge died 25th July, 1834.
> Charles Lamb died 27th Dec., 1834.
> Geo. Crabbe died 3rd Feb., 1832.
> Felicia Hemans died 16th May, 1835.

SONNETS

' In the cottage of Town-End, one afternoon in 1801, my sister read to me the sonnets of Milton. I had long been well acquainted with them, but I was particularly struck on that occasion with the dignified simplicity and majestic harmony that runs through most of them—in character so totally different from the Italian, and still more so from Shakespeare's fine sonnets. I took fire, if I may be allowed to say so, and produced three sonnets the same afternoon—the first I ever wrote, except an irregular one at school. Of these three, the only one I distinctly remember is " I grieved for Buonaparte ", &c.'

PAGE 139.   SCORN NOT THE SONNET

l. 4. *Petrarch*, Francesco (1304–1374), gave expression to his love for ' Laura ' in sonnets which have made that form of poetry the favourite vehicle of the Italian lyric.

l. 5. *Tasso*, Torquato (1544–1595), best known by his epic *La Gerusalemme Liberata*, wrote poetry of almost every sort, including the sonnet.

l. 6. *Camoens*, Luis de (1525–1580), the chief of Portuguese poets, author of *The Lusiad*, was for sixteen years an exile in the East Indies.

l. 8. *Dante*, Alighieri (1265–1321), wrote over fifty sonnets, of which half are contained in his *La Vita Nuova* (? 1292–5).

l. 10. *called from Faery-Land*. Spenser's *Amoretti* were written while he was engaged on *The Faerie Queene*.

PAGE 140. I GRIEVED FOR BUONAPARTE

The joyous welcome with which Wordsworth had hailed the Revolution (see p. 102) was damped by its excesses, and turned to abhorrence by the extinction of the Republic of Venice in May 1797, and the subjugation of the Swiss Cantons in 1798, the most conspicuous symptoms of the conversion of France from the champion to the enemy of freedom. Henceforth Napoleon is to Wordsworth the type of unscrupulous ambition, and England the bulwark of the good cause.

PAGE 140. WESTMINSTER BRIDGE

Wordsworth said, late in life, that this sonnet was ' written on the roof of a coach, on my way to France '. This statement does not agree with the date ' September 3, 1802 ' (misprinted 1803 in edd. 1807 and 1815). We know from Dorothy Wordsworth's Journal that they crossed Westminster Bridge on their way to France in the early morning of July 31. But they were back in London from August 31 to September 22. Perhaps the sonnet was cast in its final form on September 3. His sister's description of the scene is the best comment on the sonnet : ' We mounted the Dover coach at Charing Cross. It was a beautiful morning. The city, St. Paul's, with the river, and a multitude of little boats, made a most beautiful sight as we crossed Westminster Bridge. The houses were not overhung by their cloud of smoke, and they were spread out endlessly, yet the sun shone so brightly, with such a fierce light, that there was even something like the purity of one of nature's own grand spectacles.'

PAGE 141. IT IS A BEAUTEOUS EVENING

' Composed on the beach near Calais.' Wordsworth was at Calais from August 1 to August 29, 1802. His sister says in her Journal ' we walked by the sea-shore almost every evening '.

PAGE 141. EXTINCTION OF THE VENETIAN REPUBLIC

l. 8. *espouse the everlasting Sea*. In a solemn ceremony on each Ascension Day the Doge of Venice espoused the Adriatic, dropping a ring into the sea with the words, ' We espouse thee, O sea, in token of our just and perpetual dominion.'

PAGE 142.   TO TOUSSAINT L'OUVERTURE

Pierre Dominique Toussaint, surnamed L'Ouverture, was one of the leaders of the insurgent slaves in San Domingo. After the abolition of slavery was ratified by the French Government in 1793, he took service under France as Commander-in-Chief of the island, and established a firm and prosperous government. In 1801 he resisted Napoleon's edict re-establishing slavery, was captured, brought to France, and imprisoned in the castle of Joux near Besançon, where, in April 1803, he died.

PAGE 142.   SEPTEMBER 1802

The Peace of Amiens (March 1802 to May 1803) had enabled Wordsworth to pay his third visit to France, though he did not go farther than Calais. He saw that the Peace was only a short break in the long struggle. This and the two following sonnets record his feelings on landing at Dover on August 30, 1802, and during the next three weeks in London.

PAGE 144.   IT IS NOT TO BE THOUGHT OF

The quotation ' with pomp of waters, unwithstood ' is from Samuel Daniel's *Civil Wars* (1595–1609), ii. 7.   Lines 5 and 6, ' Roused . . . bands ', were substituted in 1827 for

> Road by which all might come and go that would,
> And bear out freights of worth to foreign lands.

PAGE 145.   NOVEMBER, 1806

Written on the overthrow of Prussia in the battle of Jena, October 14, 1806.   Wordsworth pointed out in a note that the two last lines are from Fulke Greville Lord Brooke's *Life of Sir Philip Sidney*—' the effeminate made judges of danger which they fear, and honor which they understand not ' (chap. viii).

PAGE 146.   CONVENTION OF CINTRA

The rising of Spain and Portugal against Napoleon in the summer of 1808 was supported by a British army under Wellesley, and followed after the victory of Vimiero (August 21) by the Convention of Cintra, under which the French army evacuated Portugal, but retained its arms, and was conveyed to France in British ships.   The largest blot upon the Convention was, as Wordsworth urged in his Tract (see p. 182), that it over rode the authority and rights and wishes of Spain and Portugal and offended the sacred principle of Nationalism. Under the dismay caused by this transaction he ' gathers triumph ' from the example of Spain.

PAGE **147.**   1811

This is the last of Wordsworth's great patriotic sonnets.
The downfall of Napoleon began in 1812, but in 1811 Wordsworth was assured of the ultimate triumph of the cause of
national freedom.

PAGE **147.**   UPON THE SIGHT OF A BEAUTIFUL PICTURE

See note on p. 28, l. 22.   The sonnet was written at the
Rectory, Grasmere, where Wordsworth resided from 1811
to 1813.   The picture belonged to him ; it was painted by
Sir George Beaumont near Coleorton.

PAGE **148.**   HAIL, TWILIGHT

See pp. 37, 38.

PAGE **148.**   AFTER-THOUGHT

An ' after-thought ' to *The River Duddon*, a series of sonnets.
The Duddon divides Cumberland and Lancashire.

l. 14.   Cf. *Paradise Lost*, viii. 282 : ' And feel that I am
happier than I know '.

PAGE **149.**   DEPARTURE OF SIR WALTER SCOTT

A memory of the evening of September 22, 1831 ; see note
on *Yarrow Revisited*, p. 133.   ' On our return in the afternoon we had to cross the Tweed directly opposite Abbotsford.
A rich, but sad, light, of rather a purple than a golden hue,
was spread over the Eildon Hills at that moment ; and, thinking it probable that it might be the last time Sir Walter would
cross the stream, I was not a little moved, and expressed some
of my feelings in the sonnet beginning " A trouble, not of clouds,
or weeping rain ".'

PREFACE TO LYRICAL BALLADS

By way of preface to the first edition of *Lyrical Ballads*, 1798,
Wordsworth contributed a short ' Advertisement ' that would
occupy only two pages of the present volume.   In the second
edition, 1800, he supplied in its place a ' Preface ' of consider-
able length on poetry in general and the principles of his own
art.   He thoroughly revised this preface for the third edition,
1802, and added to it substantially.   It must therefore be
dated ' 1800 and 1802 '.   Late in life he again revised it ; but
the changes he then made affect expression rather than matter.
It is here reprinted in its final form.

PAGE **155,** l. 25.   *frantic novels.*   He alludes to the romance
of ' Mystery and Terror ', dealing with mediaeval castles,
spectres, secret chambers, and melodramatic villains.   Mrs. Ann
Radcliffe with her *Mysteries of Udolpho* (1794) and *The Italian*
(1797), and Matthew Gregory Lewis with *The Monk* (1795)
were the chief representatives of this school.

l. 26. *German Tragedies.* Between 1797 and 1801 translations or adaptations of the plays of August von Kotzebue (1761–1819) enjoyed a furious vogue in English theatres, especially *Die Spanier in Peru,* which Sheridan adapted as *Pizarro* (1799), and *Menschenhass und Reue.*

PAGE 158, l. 1. *Gray, who was at the head of those,* &c. See Gray's letter to Richard West, April 1742 : ' As to matter of style, I have this to say : The language of the age is never the language of poetry ; except among the French, whose verse, where the thought or image does not support it, differs in nothing from prose. Our poetry, on the contrary, has a language peculiar to itself, to which almost every one that has written has added something.' Gray's observation was approved by William Mason his editor : ' nothing can be more just than this observation ; and nothing more likely to preserve our poetry from falling into insipidity '.

l. 7. *In vain to me,* &c.   Gray's *Sonnet on the Death of Richard West* (August 1742).

PAGE 159, l. 6. *tears ' such as Angels weep '. Paradise Lost,* i. 620.

l. 15. *the language of such Poetry . . . remind the Reader* (page 167, l. 29). This long and important passage was added in 1802. The sentence in 1800 ran : ' . . . distinctions which the mind voluntarily admits, I answer that the distinction of rhyme and metre is regular and uniform. . . .'

PAGE 162, l. 32. *Aristotle,* &c. *Poetics,* ix. Cf. p. 4, l. 25.

PAGE 165, l. 7. *looks before and after. Hamlet,* IV. iv. 37.

PAGE 170, l. 10. *Clarissa Harlowe,* by Samuel Richardson, 1748.

The Gamester, a tragedy by Edward Moore, produced by Garrick at Drury Lane in 1753.

PAGE 173, l. 27. *Dr. Johnson's stanza.* Johnson pronounced these verses one evening at Miss Reynolds's tea-table, when annoyed by Percy's lavish praise of the ' beautiful simplicity ' of the old ballads—Anecdotes by George Steevens published in the *European Magazine,* January 1785.

PAGE 175, l. 14. *Reynolds has observed,* in his *Seventh Discourse* (1776), on ' the reality of a Standard of Taste '.

LETTER TO LADY BEAUMONT

See note on p. 28, l. 20 and on *Elegiac Stanzas,* p. 105.

PAGE 178, l. 4. *Westminster election.* In May 1807 James Paull was a candidate for this constituency in the Radical interest with the support of Sir Francis Burdett. They quarrelled and wounded each other in a duel. Whereupon the election committee threw over Paull, and Burdett, standing in his stead, was triumphantly returned.

l. 5. *Honiton.* The contest for this borough in May 1806 is memorable as an object-lesson in electoral corruption.

PAGE 179, l. 26. ' *to Liberty.*' The group of twenty-six ' Sonnets dedicated to Liberty ', collected under this title in the edition of 1807, were all inspired by the Napoleonic war. Ten of them are given in this volume, pp. 140–5.

PAGE 180, l. 4. ' *Moods of my own Mind.*' Wordsworth gave this title to a group of thirteen poems published in 1807, including ' My heart leaps up ', *To the Cuckoo,* ' I wandered lonely as a Cloud ', and *The Small Celandine.*

THE CONVENTION OF CINTRA

The title of Wordsworth's tract runs as follows : *Concerning the Relations of Great Britain, Spain, and Portugal, to each other, and to the common enemy, at this crisis ; and specifically as affected by the Convention of Cintra : The whole brought to the test of those Principles, by which alone the Independence and Freedom of Nations can be Preserved or Recovered.*

See note on p. 209. At the point at which this extract is made Wordsworth is rebutting the contention that the Spaniards will be reconciled to the French Government by material advantages.

PAGE 182, l. 23. *Sicilian Vespers,* a name given to the rising of the Sicilians against the French on March 30, 1282, and to the massacre by which it was accompanied.

THE CLIMATE OF THE LAKE DISTRICT

Wordsworth's *Guide through the District of the Lakes in the North of England,* as it was finally named in 1835, was developed from an essay which he contributed anonymously in 1810 to *Select Views in Cumberland, Westmoreland, and Lancashire* by the Rev. Joseph Wilkinson. This essay was reprinted in the volume called *The River Duddon,* 1820, and was first published by itself as *A Description of the Scenery of the Lakes in the North of England, Third Edition,* 1822 (fourth edition, 1823). The *Guide* is the ' fifth edition '.

The second paragraph of the extract was written in 1823.

PAGE 189, l. 2. *Skiey influences,—Measure for Measure,* III. i. 9.

PAGE 190, l. 32. *Buchanan,* George (1506–1582), the great Scottish humanist, acknowledged as the greatest Latin scholar and poet of his day. In conversation with his nephew and biographer Wordsworth spoke of this Ode, the *Calendae Maiae,* as ' equal in sentiment, if not in elegance, to anything in Horace ' (*Memoirs of Wordsworth,* ii. 469).